Pease Porridge:
Beyond the King's Bread

• Cooking at Fortress Niagara •
Rations to Regal,
Royalty to Republic
1726 – 1865

by
JoAnn Demler

With Illustrations
by
Clara Ritter (Fort Scenes)
Joe Lee (Military Figures)
Marbud Prozeller (Incidentals)

© Old Fort Niagara Association, Inc. 2003
Youngstown, New York
ISBN: 0-941967-23-9

Pease Porridge: Beyond the King's Bread
• Cooking at Fortress Niagara •
Rations to Regal, Royalty to Republic
1726 – 1865

by
JoAnn Demler

With Illustrations by
Clara Ritter (Fort Scenes)
Joe Lee (Military Figures)
Marbud Prozeller (Incidentals)

© Old Fort Niagara Association, Inc., 2003

ISBN: 0-941967-23-9

First Printing: June 2003

Printed in the United States of America

_ _ _ _ _ _ _ _ _ _ _ _ _ _

Cataloging Data:
Demler, JoAnn.
   *Pease Porridge: Beyond the King's Bread: Cooking at Fortress Niagara,
   Rations to Regal, Royalty to Republic, 1726-1865* / by JoAnn Demler; with
   illustrations by Clara Ritter, Joe Lee, and Marbud Prozeller.

Youngstown, New York: Old Fort Niagara Association, Inc., 2003.

112 p. : ill. ; 26 cm.

© Old Fort Niagara Association, Inc., 2003
ISNB: 0-941967-23-9

First Printing: June 2003

1. Cookery, American-History--18th century. 2. Cookery--New York
(State)--Old Fort Niagara. 3. Old Fort Niagara (N.Y.) I. Demler, JoAnn.
II. Ritter, Clara. III. Lee, Joe. IV. Prozeller, Marbud.

Illustrations, References and Notes

TX715.D45 2003
641.3454'98

Pease Porridge:

Beyond the King's Bread

• Cooking at Fortress Niagara •
Rations to Regal,
Royalty to Republic
1726 – 1865

To the memory of

Marbud Prozeller

Archaeology Department Excavator, Conservator,
Restorer, Researcher, Educator, Artist & Illustrator;
True Friend of
Old Fort Niagara,
its Dedicated Volunteers and Staff,
and the Thousands of Visitors
Who WereTouched by Her Kindness.

• Table of Contents •

TABLE OF CONTENTS

Recipes – continued . . .

• • • • • • • • • • • • • • •

The American Troops (1796-1865)*

*with the exception of that surprise return-visit the British made in December 1813...which lasted into 1815.

• • • • • • • • • • • • • • •

Other Fort Favorites

• • • • • • • • • • • • • • •

• Introduction •

The water buckets have been filled and the wood is split and stacked. In the fireplace, the fire is burning brightly. All of the ingredients for today's cooking program have been laid out and covered. Standing in the doorway of the bakehouse, waiting for the gate to open this morning, you hope to catch a cool breeze off the river. What questions will the visitors have today? Will it be, "Are you really cooking on the fire?" or "Is that real food?" This is invariably followed by, "You're not really going to eat that, are you?" Yes, we really do cook on hot summer days, and yes, the soldiers really do eat eat the foods we prepare.

The Old Fort Niagara cooking program was established by Mary Catherine Hallatt and Lynn M. Lipa in the spring of 1982. In the 1990's, a small garden on the riverside of the bakehouse was added. The program is intended to acquaint our visitors with the types of food eaten by those at the fort during the eighteenth and early nineteenth centuries. In the use of open hearth cooking, interpreters demonstrate many of the methods used to prepare these foods. The cooking program centers on the foodstuffs available during those times. In 1986 Mary and Lynn compiled a cookbook for the fort which was entitled *The King's Bread: Eighteenth Century Cooking at Niagara*. As new research became available in 1989, Carol and Dennis Farmer did a revision with their book *The King's Bread, 2nd Rising*. As we are always learning new things about such an old place (the French Castle is over 275 years old!), it is time, once again, to revise and expand the *Cooking at Niagara Cookbook*. The format of the book remains the same with French, British and American periods but we have added Native American and German recipes as well as some of our favorites.

Recipes of the eighteenth century were not as precise as those found in the cookbooks of today. The measurement of ingredients was often vague or not given at all. Recipes were generally descriptions of what to do rather than step-by-step directions. The following recipe for "potato cake" from Amelia Simmons' 1796 *American Cookery* is not atypical:

> *Boil potatoes, peel* [sic] *and pound them,*
> *add yolks of eggs, wine and melted butter work*
> *with flour into paste, shape as you please, bake*
> *and pour over them melted butter, wine and sugar.*[1]

The recipes included in this cookbook have been drawn from many sources, both eighteenth & nineteenth century, as well as modern. Every effort has been made to adjust the recipes for the modern kitchen and conventional oven. However, cooking is meant to be enjoyed and we encourage you not to be afraid to experiment with these recipes (as we have). They should act as a guide for which you eliminate ingredients you don't like and add those you do. Eighteenth century cooking, was less structured than today, so go ahead and have fun!

• FRENCH OCCUPATION •
1726-1759

Fort Niagara was established by Gaspard Chaussegros de Léry and a small detachment of soldiers of the *Compagnies Franches de la Marine* in 1726. This fort was the third to be built at the mouth of the Niagara River. The earliest French posts proved to be difficult to maintain because of the distance from French settlements on the St. Lawrence River and the hostility of the local Iroquois Indians. The first, Fort Conte, was constructed in 1679 as a trading post for the explorer, René-Robert Cavelier, Sieur de la Salle. This small outpost was burned and abandoned soon after its establishment. Fort Denonville was the second post to be built at this site in 1687. This wooden stockade was home to one hundred soldiers, most of whom were to lose their lives during the winter of 1687-88. The twelve that remained were rescued and taken away by a relief party in the spring, leaving the fort to rot. The third Fort Niagara was a well defended citadel comprised of a stone "Castle" and a four bastioned stockade. Within this stronghold, storerooms provided shelter for provisions and a *"boulangerie"* or bakery for the garrison. Officers had a *"cabinet au cuisine"* or kitchen in which to prepare their meals and a *"chambre au cuisine"* or dining room in which to take their meals. The enlisted soldiers prepared and ate their simple fare in a "corps de garde" or barracks room, using an open fireplace and eating at a communal table. [2]

The normal ration for the soldiers of the
Compagnies Franches de la Marine
during the eighteenth century was:

3/4 lb meat per day (salt beef, salt pork, bacon)
2 lbs peas per week
6 lb loaf of bread baked every four days [3]

In the 1500s, a steaming bowl of porridge was the daily fare for a poor peasant. Even though they planted, grew and harvested the grains themselves, they would not have been able to afford to have it ground into flour for bread or baking. Even if they were able to attain flour they would have no means for baking bread and other products as most peasants had no oven. Nutritious and filling, the whole grains which included dried peas, were cooked slowly and cautiously in a large pot. They would add the seasonal vegetables and herbs they grew in their gardens, along with the occasional chunk of salted meat. Folks would eat this porridge for days, leaving any leftovers in the pot to get cold overnight before rekindling the fire for the next meal. Some times the stew had food in it that had been there for days. Hence, the nursery rhyme. [4]

• • • • • • •

Most soldiers at Fort Niagara cooked their own food in a group of men known as a "mess".

A mess usually consisted of five to six soldiers who shared a pot, a room and cooking chores.

The kettle or pot was the most versatile cooking implement. It was made of iron, usually as deep or deeper than it was wide, with short legs for balance. It was then, either suspended over the fire by hooks or set on a trivet. It might or might not have had a lid. These are a very good choice for cooking soups, stews, puddings, roasts and custards.[6] A properly seasoned cast iron pot will enhance the flavor of your cooking. Wash the pot with a mild soap and dry. Apply unsalted vegetable oil* to the inside of the pot.

Then hang it over the fire or place it in an oven (approximately 250°) for two hours. Wipe the pot with more oil twice during the drying period. The first few times a newly seasoned pot is used, it is best to cook fatty foods. Then use it for stews or vegetables. Always use a mild soap to clean cast iron ware. Avoid scouring as it will remove the protective seasoning and should be reseasoned for best use. It rust appears on a pot or food has a metallic taste, it is also an indication that the pot needs to be reseasoned. *We found that vegetable oil gets sticky. Other sources say to use vegetable shortening. However, we have found that using mineral oil is best because it doesn't get sticky nor does it get rancid if the pot is not used. This same method can be used for any of your iron cookware-frying pans, Dutch ovens, etc.

Pease Porridge

Pease porridge hot,
Pease porridge cold,
Pease porridge in the pot nine days old.

Some like it hot,
Some like it cold,
Some like it in the pot nine days old.

Pease soup or pease porridge was the daily provision cooked by the common soldier. It would have been made by simply throwing the dried peas and meat together in a large kettle, along with any vegetables available and enough water to cook them properly. The recipe which follows was handed down from the first Cooking at Niagara cookbook, "The King's Bread."

• • • • • • • • • •

Pease Soup [5]
Officers' & Common Fare

1/2 lb split peas
1/4 lb salt pork
1 meaty ham bone
1 medium onion, diced
1/2 cup carrots, diced
1/2 tsp dry mustard
1/8 tsp ground savory
3 whole cloves
3/4 tsp salt
1/2 tsp pepper

Cover peas with 4 inches of water. Add other ingredients and bring to a boil. Turn down the heat and let simmer for 2 hours or until peas are cooked.
• *Cook's Note:* Start the pot by dicing the pork salt (for which you can substitute bacon or ham) and frying it along with the onion and 1-2 cloves of garlic to enhance the flavor. We have also added fresh herbs from the garden and a bay leaf while simmering.

Le Pain or Bread [7]
Officers' & Common Fare

6 cups room temperature water
2 Tbl dry yeast
2 Tbl salt
16-18 cups flour (approximately 4 cups stones ground rye
    flour and 12 cups stone ground whole wheat flour)

First you make the "sponge" by mixing together in a large bowl 6 cups of water, 2 Tbl yeast and 6-8 cups of flour and beating for 100 strokes; cover and let rise for 1/2 hour. Beat down and fold in 2 Tbl salt; add remaining flour, one cup at a time, until the dough comes away from the sides of the bowl. Turn out on floured surface and knead until smooth, at least 15 minutes. Use additional flour if necessary. Place in a greased bowl. Turn dough so that the entire surface is oiled. Cover and place in a draft-free area. Allow to rise until doubled in bulk. Punch down and allow to rise again in the same manner. Turn dough out on a floured surface and knead 4-5 minutes. Divide into four equal portions. Shape into rounds and place on greased cookie sheets, 3-4 inches apart. Allow to rise again, 20-30 minutes. Bake in a preheated oven for 400° for 20 minutes, reduce to 350° and continue to bakes for 45 minutes longer or until loaf sounds hollow when tapped on.

Today we are fortunate enough to have packaged yeast readily available for use. The process of "starting" bread that was leavened was discovered centuries ago. By allowing flour and water to ferment, the natural yeasts from the air would grow and cause bread to rise. In order to have that occur one might have used the following recipe:

Natural Starter
- 150 gm whole rye flour (10 1/2 ounces which is a lttile more than 2 cups)
- 150 gm whole wheat flour which was bolted (unbleached flour)
- 300 gm room temperature water (10 1/2 ounces which is a little more than 1 1/4 cup)
- 3 gm salt (a little less than 1 tsp)
- 3 gm malt

Mix together in a bowl or crock until well blended and let it sit out for 22 hours (the volume wil have doubled). Take out 300 gm of the mixture (discard the rest) and add to it 150 rye flour, 150 unbleached flour, 150 gm water, 1 gm salt, 2 gm malt and let sit another 7 hours (it will have tripled in size). Once again take out 300 gm of mixture and discard the rest. Add to this 150 gm rye flour, 150 gm unbleached flour, 150 gm water and let it sit for 7 hours. Repeat this process three more times, only letting the "start" sit for 6 hours each time. When this is completed, you use this mixture 25 parts of starter to 100 parts of flour, in other words 1:4. This process gives you what we know today as a "sourdough" bread. [8]

Bread was the mainstay of the soldier's ration at Fort Niagara. This recipe is appropriate for British and United States troops as well. It was prepared by the garrison baker. Bread for the garrison was baked in large quantities. When Fort Niagara was first occupied by the French after 1726, baking was done in the "boulangerie", now called the "French Kitchen", on the first floor of the "Castle". During the 1740's the French garrison built a wooden bakehouse separate from the Castle. It contains a pair of brick-lined ovens. Each was heated by building a large fire in the oven cavity. Smoke escaped through the oven door and was drawn up the building's single chimney. As the bricks of the oven became hot, they turned a pinkish white, indicating that the temperature was high enough to bake. Sprinkling flour on the bricks was another way for the garrison baker to determine if the oven was ready. If the flour turned brown within three to five seconds, the temperature was right for baking. The coals and embers were then scraped out the door and deposited on the hearth. Bread dough was placed inside the oven by means of a wooden shovel called a "peel" much like the ones used in pizza ovens today. These loaves were not baked in pans, but were placed directly on the hot bricks. Two doors, one wooden and the other metal, sealed the opening. The length of baking time varied according to the oven's temperature. Forty to fifty loaves could be baked at a time in each oven, and two to three batches of bread could be baked before the ovens needed to be refired.[9]

"Starter" Bread
Common Fare

A much simpler recipe which relies on packaged yeast for "starting" bread is as follows:

Mix 1 cup of flour with 1 cup of room temperature water and a pinch of yeast. Stir until well blended. Leave this mixture alone for 7 days in a large glass or plastic container, unrefrigerated. To keep this "starter" going so that it is always readily available for use, use some of the starter or discard 1/2 cup of it and stir together equal amounts of flour and water and add to mixture until smooth and creamy. You may store this at room temperature or refrigerate. However, before using it you should bring it up to room temperature.

2 cups "starter" at room temperature
1 pkg dry yeast (this will make rising faster)
3 Tbl melted fat (butter, lard, etc.)
4 cups flour
2 Tbl sugar
1 tsp salt

Place flour, sugar and salt in a large mixing bowl. Stir together starter yeast and melted fat. Mix liquid with dry until well blended. Turn out on floured board and knead for 10-15 minutes. Place in well-greased bread pan or form into round loaf and place on well greased cookie tin. Let rise for about 2 hours in warm place until doubled. Bake in Dutch oven (350º) for 50-60 minutes.

Ash Cake or Fire Cake [10]
Common Fare

1 lb flour
water
salt

Mix the flour and a little salt (if you have it) with the water until a thick, damp dough is made. Mold it in the cup of your hand, into a flat cake. Place in ashes of your fire, atop a rock, if possible. Bake for half an hour or until blackened. Remove, cool and eat.

• • • • • • • • •

Sagamite or *Bouillon de Gru* [12]
Common Fare

1 cup white corn meal
1/2 lb whitefish
2 quarts water

Boil whitefish in one cup of water and break up fish. In a separate pot, boil corn meal (gru) in water until it takes on a gruel-like consistency. When this gruel is about half cooked, add the fish. Stir briskly and complete cooking.

• • • • • • • • •

Gagaitetaakwa or Boiled Corn Bread [14]
Common Fare

1 cup fine corn meal (Indian corn)
3/4 cup boiling water
1/4 cup cranberries
pot of boiling water

Mix corn meal with 3/4 cup boiling water. Stir in cranberries. Form into a round, flattened loaf. Rinse hands in cold water and rub outside of loaf to give a shiny appearance. Drop into a pot of boiling water. Make sure the pot is big enough so that the loaf does not touch the sides. Cook one hour or until loaf floats. You may also bake it buried under the ashes, with a fire above.

When out on campaign, soldiers were only issued flour to keep their packs light. Captain Pouchot accounts that each soldier and officer were given 30 pounds of flour along with the other provisions needed for fighting. "As a result the army could last for a whole month without recourse to supplies. Both soldiers and officers mixed some flour with a little water. They kneaded it and cooked it into cakes on a stone or under embers. This arrangement was very good for a light expedition." [11]

Cooking fires were started with flint and steel. It is still a challenge to start the fire using this method. Flint is a very hard gray or brown stone which will generate sparks when struck against steel. These sparks are struck onto a piece of charred fabric, better known to us as "charcloth". Once the fabric had begun to smolder, it is carefully placed on a nest made of flax tow or unraveled twine. Flax tow is the outside fibers of flax. This soon bursts into flames which is carefully fed with small pieces of tinder, shavings or bark. Birch bark works best of all because of its natural oils and papery texture. After this, smaller pieces of kindling should be put carefully on the fire. It is important to have the proper hardwood for baking and cooking. Maple, ash and oak are the best. It takes at least 30 minutes to get suitable coals for cooking but that doesn't mean you can't put on the kettle for hot water.

• • • • • • •

The name "sagamite" was translated by Antoine Laumet, de Lamothe, sieur de Cadillac, founder of Detroit, in his 1718 "Relation" to mean, "a variety of things mixed together to be eaten." As the name denotes, many other types of fish and wild plant could be used to complete this simple, yet filling meal.

This was a common Native American food which the earliest Jesuit missionaries traveling in North America came upon. "A Porridge made of the meal of Indian corn and water, morning and evenings, and for a drink a flagon of water. Sometimes the savages put in pieces of cinders, to season the sagamite, at other times a handful of little waterflies, which are like the gnats of Provence; they esteem these highly, make feast of them. The more prudent keep some fish after fishing season to break into the sagamite during the year, about half of a carp is put in for fourteen persons, and the more tainted the fish is, the better. [13]

Since much game and wild fowl was eaten by Niagara's French garrison, it is included here. It is listed, according to Barbara Ketcham Wheaton, in "Les Dons de Comus" of 1758. It was the "bouillon ordinare" which provided the basis for many different dishes. Peter Kalm, a Swedish naturalist who visited the post in the autumn of 1750 noted, "Both Indians and resident French soldiers from Fort Niagara are said to appear here (below Niagara Falls) daily to gather the supply of sea fowls (swept over the cataract). The birds were said to make good food if they had not been dead too long. [16]

Bouillon Ordinare [15]
Officers' & Common Fare

4 lbs beef
1 boiling fowl (chicken)
2 onions
3 leeks
1 oz parsley
1 whole clove
salt to taste

In a large kettle, add 1 gallon of water to the beef and chicken. Slowly bring to a gentle boil. Skim off all the floating matter and foam as it cooks. When no more comes up, add the onions with the clove stuck into it, leeks and parsley. Continue gently simmering. Remove the chicken when it is done. By the time the beef is done, so is the *bouillon.* This will take about 5 hours. Strain and cool. Discard the fat that solidified on the top. This is a good soup as is but is intended to serve as a broth to many other dishes. Game, birds, and red meat may all be cooked in this *bouillon.* Avoid using cabbage and root vegetables with this but any other greens are good in it.

• *Cook's Note:* The leeks of today are not the ones referred to in this recipe. In the woods of the Niagara region, one can still pull leeks or wild onions, to use in cooking. They are much stronger and give a more definite flavor. Onions, leeks, garlic and garlic are all native to North America but were more commonly used for medicinal purposes.

• • • • • • • • •

Baked Fish [17]
Common Fare

With water all around, fish would have been bountiful for the French. Peter Kalm, during his visit to Niagara Falls, recounted, "Sometimes, in fact almost daily, fishes suffer the same fate (going over the falls)." Kalm also described bear, deer and bird being collected at the foot of the falls. The commandant of Fort Niagara, Captain Daniel Lienard de Beaujeu, reported that, in the autumn, his men lived on this bountiful crop. [18]

1 whole fish, cleaned

Make a smooth bed of hot coals from the fire. Cover the coals with white ashes. Lay gutted fish on ashes and cover completely with more white ashes. Finally, cover everything with more hot coals from the fire. Bake 2 minutes for each inch.

Eels *aux Trois Rivieres* [19]
Common Fare

2 lbs eel
8 oz butter
1 large onion or leek, finely diced
2 shallots, finely diced
salt & pepper to taste
1 gill sorrel or spinach (1/2 cup), chopped
1 gill watercress (1/2 cup), chopped
1/3 oz parsley, chopped
sage, savory and mint, minced
wine or cider
1/2 gill vinegar (1/4 cup)
1/2 oz flour
1 egg yolk

Remove the skin and backbone of eel. Cut into 2 or 3 inch sections. Fry lightly with butter and onion and shallots. Season to taste. Add sorrel or spinach, watercress and parsley. Cook rapidly for some 10 to 15 minutes, then add enough wine or cider to cover the eel. In a bowl, mix the egg yolk, flour and vinegar with the eel's broth to make a sauce. Care must be given to avoid curdling. Pour sauce over eels and serve. Dish may be served hot or cold.

• • • • • • • • •

Fried Muskrat [21]
Common Fare

1 muskrat
2 medium onions, chopped
salt and pepper

Skin and remove the musk gland from the 'rat. Immerse it in a kettle of water. Add onions. Salt and pepper to taste. Cook until scum is no longer produced. Drain off water, leaving onion with the muskrat. Add more water and continue cooking until tender. Remove and fry as you like in a skillet or spider.

Cook's Note: Soak the cleaned muskrat in salt water with 2 Tbl of vinegar for 2 hours. Drain, rinse and then proceed.

After Peter Kalm visited Fort Niagara, in 1750, detailed in his Travels that "Among other fish they catch are a large number of small eels of nine or twelve inches in length, and all the dexterity needed for their capture is to go below the cataract (Niagara Falls) and feel around with the fingers in the cracks, holes and crevices of the wet rock, find and grab them." [20]

Frying was typically done in a spider. A spider is shaped like a frying pan with long legs, allowing it to stand over the fire. When doing open hearth cooking, you adjust the temperature by moving your cooking utensils or manipulating the fire. One simply can move the kettle up or down, the spider farther or closer to the coals, or add or remove coals from the fire.

Muskrat was (and still is, by some) considered a delicacy by the French inhabitants of the Great Lakes. This small game animal lives in marshy areas and has a strong but tasty flesh. The musk gland must be removed before cooking, however. If the gland is left in, the muskrat will taste as if it were allowed to rot! French garrisons, including those of Fort Niagara and Michilimackinac, have left large numbers of muskrat bones about their sites. [22]

Captain Marin de la Malgue, while supervising the movement of troops and equipment across the Niagara Portage, reported on May 24, 1753, that many of his voyageurs had not had any soup for three days owing to lack of salt pork. He requested a supply from Fort Niagara. Marin evidently looked forward to the meal as he wrote on May 26, "I am very much obliged to you, sir, for what you have sent me to make soup with, and I can assure you it will be good. All these gentlemen will enjoy it with me." [24]

Potage de Chair (Salt Pork Soup) [23]
Officers' & Common Fare

2 lbs salt pork
vinegar
salt and pepper
2 lbs stale bread, cut into two inch pieces
2 lbs mixed vegetables (turnips, cabbage, carrots, parsnips), diced

Soak the salt pork for two hours in a kettle of water. Throw away the water and wash again. Cut into one-inch cubes. In a frying pan, heat a little fat until melted and then add cubes of pork, brown well. Boil a kettle of water. Add the pork and boil for 15 minutes. Add vegetables and cook for 90 minutes. Add in a little vinegar and salt and pepper to taste. Add cubed bread and cook for 15 minutes more. Remove any fat that floats to the surface before serving.

Cook's Note: Salt pork was not the salt pork we think of as today- a type of bacon that is smoked. It was simply pork that was preserved in a heavy brine of salt water. It was the most typical meat sent to Fort Niagara (and eaten by all three armies; French, British and American).

• • • • • • • • •

Ciselette or **Salt Pork and Molasses Sauce** [25]
Officers' Fare

1/2 cup salt or fresh pork, in cubes
1 cup molasses

If using salt pork, boil it in a frying pan with a small amount of water for 2-3 minutes to remove the salt. Pour off the water and fry the pork in its own fat until golden brown. Remove from the pan and set aside. Add the molasses to the remaining pork fat and simmer gently for several minutes. When the mixture begins to boil, remove the pan from the heat and add the pork fat pieces. Serve hot or cold with fresh white bread.

Tourtiere (French Canadian Pork Pie) [26]
Officers' Fare

 2 lbs ground pork
1 1/4 cups chopped onion
2/3 cup water
salt & pepper to taste
1 tsp cinnamon
3/4 tsp ground cloves
3/4 tsp ground nutmeg
1 Tbl flour
1/4 cup cold water
pie crust (see below)

Combine pork, and onion in a skillet and brown. Add water, salt, pepper, cinnamon, cloves and nutmeg and simmer for 20 minutes. Meanwhile stir flour and 1/4 cup cold water until there are no lumps. When meat mixture is ready, stir in flour mixture, bring to boil and thicken.

Pastry shell for 10 inch pie

2 cups flour
1/2 tsp salt
1/2 cup lard
4-6 Tbl cold water
1 egg , well beaten

Mix flour and salt together in large bowl. Cut in lard until the mixture has the consistency of coarse cornmeal. Add water a little at a time. When blended divide in half and form two balls. Roll the dough on a well floured surface. Place into pie tin. Add meat mixture. Place top crust on carefully and make 1/2 inch slits to allow pie to vent. Brush with egg. Bake at 425º for 10 minutes, and then lower heat to 350º. Bake 40 minutes or until crust is brown. This may also be served cold topped with real maple syrup.

When baking single items or if a brick or bake oven was not available, baking kettles, better known as Dutch ovens, were used. There were made of iron, usually not as deep as a kettle, with short legs and a tightly fitted, flanged lid. They could be used in the place of a kettle for soups and stews. When Dutch ovens are used for baking the lid and oven should be preheated before food is placed inside. A pile of coals should be placed on the side of the hearth, away from the fire, and the Dutch oven set directly on the coals. The food should then be placed inside the oven, the lid put in place, and additional hot coals evenly placed on the lid. It might be necessary to change the coals several times before an item has finished baking. Changing coals allows you to maintain a consistent cooking temperature. If it is not possible to keep the Dutch oven away from the regular fire, make sure you rotate the oven so one side does not get hotter than the other. The Dutch oven should be slightly larger than the item you wish to bake to allow air space for better baking. The pie, cake or bread should not touch the sides. If you are using the Dutch oven as the pan, make sure it is well-seasoned. If you are placing a pan inside the oven, use a trivet underneath to give it air space underneath for more even baking.

When cooking in a pot over the fire the simplest method to raise or lower the temperature is to raise or lower the pot. This is done by using a trammel and adjusting the hook or using a set of S-hooks. By adding or taking away S-hooks you can raise or lower the pot.

Cretons or French-Canadian Pork Spread [27]
Officers' Fare

1/2 lb salt pork, diced
1 lb pork, cut up
1 large onion, quartered
1/4 tsp ground cloves
1/2 tsp ground cinnamon
1/8 tsp ground allspice
1/8 tsp pepper
1/4 cup fine dry bread crumbs

Cook salt pork in spider or skillet until crisp and golden brown. Drain and reserve 1/4 cup of drippings. Grind together the salt pork, pork and onions. Return to the spider, add drippings, cloves, cinnamon, allspice, and pepper. Cover and cook over low heat for 15-20 minutes stirring occasionally. Remove from the heat. Stir in the bread crumbs. Turn mixture into a bowl, cover and chill. Serve on bread.

• • • • • • • • •

Onion Soup
Common & Officers' Fare

6-8 onions, peeled and sliced
1/2 cup butter
1/4 cup flour
2 cups beef stock or bouillon
4 cups water

Heat butter in a pot until melted. Stir in onions and cook slowly until they are transparent. Sprinkle flour over onions and stir until golden brown. Slowly add stock and water. Simmer for approximately one hour. If desired, top soup with slices of dried bread and cheese. Cover until cheese melts.

Biscuits de Chocolat [28]
Officers' Fare

2 oz unsweetened chocolate, grated
8 oz sugar (1 cup)
4 egg yolks
8 egg whites, stiffly beaten
4 oz flour (1/2 cup)

Beat the grated chocolate, sugar and egg yolks in a bowl until thick and creamy. Add the stiffly beaten egg whites. Sift the flour over the mix and gently fold it in. Spoon about 2 ounces into lightly greased custard cups. Bake in at 325º for 15-20 minutes. Remove when tops are just firm. Cool before serving. Black pepper and cinnamon may be added in small amounts for a more 18th century taste.

• • • • • • • • •

Pain Perdu (**French Toast**)
Officers' Fare

8 slices day old bread (French bread, sliced about one inch thick is wonderful!)
2 eggs, well beaten
2/3 cup milk
2 Tbl powdered sugar
dash of salt
1/2 tsp vanilla
cinnamon
margarine or shortening for frying
powdered sugar, honey or maple syrup

Combine eggs, milk, powdered sugar, salt and vanilla in a wide bowl with room to soak bread slices. Soak bread slices, coating both sides, drain excess liquid and sprinkle with cinnamon. Heat a skillet or griddle and add margarine or shortening for frying. Gently place slice in skillet and fry over medium heat , turning once to lightly brown both sides. Sprinkle with powdered sugar and serve hot. Also may be served with honey or maple syrup.

This recipe was taken from "La Science du maitre d'hotel, confiseur" *dated 1750. Chocolate has long been a misunderstood part of eighteenth century cuisine. Surprisingly large quantities of chocolate are found in the accounts of the French and Indian War and later. At Niagara , references are given for chocolate as a drink used by many people. Interestingly enough, Indians, common traders, rangers and prisoners were all listed as users of this delicious foodstuff.* [29]

"Pain perdu" *is the French for "lost bread" and is a perfect way to use up stale bread.*

French Biscuits [30]
Officers' Fare

2 cups lukewarm water
1 Tbl sugar
1 Tbl dry yeast
7 cups sifted flour

pinch of salt
1/2 cup lard
2 eggs, well beaten

Mix the water, sugar and yeast together. Let stand about 10 minutes. Stir flour and salt together, cut in lard until well mixed. Add eggs to yeast mixture and then add to flour mixture to make the dough. Let rise about 45 minutes. Punch down, roll out on well-floured board, cut out with floured biscuit cutter. Place on greased baking sheet, 2-3 inches apart. Cover and let rise until double again. Bake at 400° until golden brown about 10-12 minutes. Serve these with butter and maple syrup for a real treat.

• • • • • • • • •

Herbes Salees or Salted Herbs [31]

1 onion, finely chopped
4 cups chives, shallots or onion shoots, cut into 1/2 inch pieces
1/2 cup coarse salt

Layer the ingredients in a stoneware or glass crock. Let the mixture stand for several days until a brine is formed. This is used as a basic ingredient in fricot, soups and most dishes which use fish and meat.

• • • • • • • • •

Soup au chou or Cabbage Soup [32]
Common Fare

1/2 cup salt pork, cut into small pieces
1 small onion, chopped
10 cups water or beef broth
salt and pepper

1 small cabbage, chopped
Optional-1 cup of diced turnips
1 Tbl salted herbs (see recipe before)

To remove the salt from the pork, let salt pork boil for 2-3 minutes in a small amount of water. Drain the pork and sauté it until lightly browned. Add the water or beef broth along with the cabbage, salted herbs and onion. Simmer at low heat for about 1 1/2 hours, or until cabbage is transparent. During the last 30 minutes, season with salt and pepper.

Soupe au pain or Bread Soup [33]
Officers' & Common Fare

1/4 cup salt pork, in cubes
1 Tbl salted herbs
1 onion, chopped
1 cup milk

2 slices day-old bread, cut into small pieces
salt and pepper
3 cups beef broth

Boil the salt pork in a small amount ot water; drain and sauté until lightly browned. Add the onions and continue to sauté the mixture until the onion is golden brown. Add the bread to the pot and stir for a few minutes. Add the broth and the salted herbs and bring it to a boil. Add the milk and season to taste. Remove the soup from the heat and let it stand for a few minutes before serving.

Cook's Note: You may use croutons of dry bread in place of the day-old bread. You may also replace the broth with milk-part of it or all of it.

• • • • • • • • •

Poutine au pain or Bread Pudding [34]
Officers' Fare

1 cup milk
1/4 tsp salt
2 cups stale bread, cut into small pieces
1/2 cup sugar

2 eggs, beaten
2 Tbl butter
1 tsp vanilla

Optional: Stir in 1/2 cups of raisins or 1 cup blueberries or 1 cup of diced apples to the mixture just before baking.

Heat the milk and pour is over the bread. In a separate bowl, mix together the eggs, vanilla, salt, sugar and butter. Blend in the milk and bread. Pour into a greased pan and bake at 350° for approximately 1 hour. Serve hot with *Sauce au sucre brun. (see below)*

• • • • • • • • •

Sauce au sucre brun or Brown Sugar Sauce [35]

1 cup brown sugar
1 1/4 cups cold water
4 tsp flour

1 tsp vanilla
dash of salt
1 Tbl butter

Mix the sugar, flour and salt together into a medium-sized pan. Add the water and bring mixture to a boil; stirring constantly until the sauce thickens and becomes syrupy. Remove from the hear, and allow it to cool slightly. Add the butter and the vanilla.

Riz aux raisins or Rice Pudding [36]
Officers' Fare

2 cups water   1 cup rice
1 Tbl butter   3/4 cup raisins
1/2 tsp salt   1/2 cup milk
1/4 cup sugar

Place the water in a medium-sized pan and bring it to a boil. Add the salt and rice. Cover and simmer for 20 minutes or until the rice is cooked. Add the remaining ingredients and simmer for 25 minutes. Serve with *Suace au sucre brun*. (see Page 21)

• • • • • • • • •

Rabbit Pie [37]
Officers' Fare

8 slices bacon or fresh salt pork   3 potatoes, peeled and sliced
salt and pepper   3 leeks, chopped into 1 inch slices
1 bay leaf   1 Tbl vinegar
3 Tbl chopped parsley   1 rabbit, cut into small portions
1 lb mushrooms, sliced

In the bottom of pot or Dutch oven, place bay leaf, 4 slices of bacon, 1/2 of mushrooms and leeks. Put rabbit in and cover with layers of remaining mushrooms and leeks. Add salt, pepper and parsley. Put potatoes on top, sprinkle with salt and add remaining bacon. Pour vinegar over the top. Cover and bake at 350° for 2 hours. Keep covered to retain juices. Serve warm.

• • • • • • • • •

Soupe au bele D'inde or Corn Soup [38]
Officers' & Common Fare

3 cups potatoes, diced   3 cups water, salted
2 Tbl butter   salt and pepper to taste
1 1/2 cups corn kernels (fresh or other) 1 large onion, chopped
2 cups milk   1 Tbl butter

Boil the potatoes in salted water until tender, about 15 minutes. Cook the corn also, if using fresh corn. Saute the onion in 2 Tbl butter. Add the milk and heat until warm. Add the potatoes, corn and cooking liquid. Season to taste. Just before serving, add 1 Tbl butter.

Roast Beaver [39]
Officers' & Common Fare

1 beaver   1-2 large onions, sliced
6 slices bacon   salt and pepper

Optional: Add potatoes, carrots, rutabagas, parsnips or turnips to the roasting pan like a pot roast.

Place prepared beaver in a roasting pan. Cover with slices onions and bacon. Add salt and pepper. Bake at 325º until tender.

Cook's Note: Beaver is a very red, dark meat with a strong flavor. To prepare it, thaw it or let it set if fresh with a cup of vinegar and 2 tablespoons of salt in a bowl of water. This will draw off the blood. Beaver have several musk glands which must be removed or the meat will smell like skunk. Use a sharp knife to remove any white tissue, including all fat. Place the meat in a kettle of water, with a tablespoon of baking soda. Heat and skim off the foam as it cooks. From this point the beaver may be treated like any other red meat.

• • • • • • • • •

Fried Beaver Tail [40]
Officers' & Common Fare

To prepare the tail for use, because it is very difficult to skin, simply roast it slowly on a spit over the fire. The heat on the hot fat causes the skin to split making it easy to peel. Dredge the slices of tail in seasoned flour and fry until tender in hot fat.

• • • • • • • • •

Les Croquignoles or French Crullers [41]
Officers' Fare

4 well-beaten eggs   1 tsp cinnamon
2 tsp salt   1/2 cup milk
4 Tbl melted lard   1 tsp nutmeg
4 tsp baking powder (pearl ash)   4 cups flour
1 cup sugar   Hot melted lard or oil for frying

Combine well beaten eggs, sugar, milk and melted, cooled lard. Sift together dry ingredients. Mix well with egg mixture. Knead gently. Pat or roll out to 1/2 inch thickness. Cut about 1 1/2 inches long and 1 inch wide. Give a slight twist and drop into hot lard. Cook until light brown, drain on paper and roll in either granulated or powdered sugar. Crullers are best served hot.

• BRITISH OCCUPATION •
Pre-Revolutionary War 1759-1775

In July 1759, after a thirteen day battle, the British were to seize Fort Niagara from the French. As soon as the smoke cleared from the siege, it became very apparent that the bombardment left Fort Niagara in a sorry state of repair. Not only were the Flag Bastion breached, the earthworks torn down and buildings damaged but the French-prepared gardens were in ruins. The importance of the fresh fruits and vegetables to supplement the daily rations quickly became evident. That winter, of the 600 British soldiers who were left to garrison the fort, 149 of them were to perish from scurvy, a nutritional disorder caused by the lack of Vitamin C.

On February 6, 1760, Lieutenant Colonel William Eyre reported to Lieutenant Colonel Frederick Haldimand, then at Oswego, that his situation had become critical In addition to the use of fruits and vegetables to prevent this, "spruce beer" was also used. Lacking the necessary produce, Eyre tried to brew spruce beer. The "beer" was easily made with molasses, water and spruce branches. However, Fort Niagara was also without molasses. With scurvy striking 270 of the men, the fort surgeon was forced to concoct another curative. It was too late, this new brew could not stop the disorder. Only the opening of the lake in the spring of 1750 halted this epidemic as molasses, lime and lemon juice were rushed to the fort.

A hard lesson was learned. From then on, the garrison of Fort Niagara would expand its food resources. In the spring of 1760, Eyre made sure that a large quantity of garden seed was forwarded. Crops included beets, peas, carrots, beans, onions. cabbage, turnips and greens. Potatoes were available but not well accepted by the British until later. They were not grown at the fort until the time of the American Revolution (1775-83). Fruit trees were also grown between the French Castle and Lake Ontario (a place that is no longer there, due to erosion). Cherries and peaches were so plentiful that they were sent to other places. Nets were sent to allow the men to trap passenger pigeons and lake fish. A brewery for the production of spruce beer was added to the trader's village, known as "the Bottom". Efforts were made to prevent waste, although sometimes it impossible.[1]

Shipping salt pork down the St. Lawrence is a prime example of this. It was shipped in 215 pound barrels from Europe to Quebec. After inspection, and sometimes repacking to a smaller container, the meat was loaded aboard small river craft such as canoes or bateaux. Canadian boatmen or soldiers, who were poorly paid and overworked, manned the bateaux. They had to stop and carry or "portage" the loads around the many rapids along the St. Lawrence River in order to get their cargoes here. A simple trick was to drain the salt brine from the barrels and steal the salt, to lighten their load. When they got close to Fort Niagara, they would refill the casks with fresh water to restore the weight. Those barrels were stored until needed. Many times the barrels would be opened to find long-spoiled meat.[2] On April 25, 1762, deputy commissioner Neil Maclean wrote to Major William Walters, commandant of Niagara, that:

> *I find the Bungs of almost all the Pork Barrels has been knocked out*
> *& the pickle lost,-of Five Hundred Barrels of Pork now in Store,*
> *there is not above Seventy of them, has any Pickle in them.*[3]

The basic ration of the British soldier changed but little at Fort Niagara from 1759-1775. For seven days, one man was allowed:

7 pounds of bread or flour, 4 pounds of salt pork, 3 pints of "pease,"
6 ounces of butter and 1/2 pint of rice. Sometimes a ration would
vary to account for "overplusses" or deficiencies.[4]

Ration Stew [5]
Common Fare

1 lb salt pork (fresh pork may be used to suit modern tastes)
1/2 lb dried peas and/or rice
fresh or dried vegetables according to season

Brown the salt pork and cook in a pot of water for one-half hour. If using peas, let them soak in water ahead of time until they swell. Dried peas take longer to cook than do fresh peas, so they should be added to the pot at the same time as the pork. If using rice, add it directly to the boiling water to avoid clumping. Fresh or dried vegetables should be added later. Simmer until done – about 2-3 hours. Herbs and spices such as parsley, thyme and rosemary could be added from the fort's gardens for flavoring.

• • • • • • • • •

Spruce Beer [6]
Common Fare

4 oz hops
1/2 gallon molasses
2-4 oz essence of spruce
2 oz yeast
water

Make essence of spruce by boiling young, tender sprigs of spruce in 3 gallons of water for 3 hours. Strain the mixture and discard the spruce. Add new spruce to the kettle with the liquid and repeat the process by boiling it again for 3 hours. Do this process one more time. Strain and save the liquid essence of spruce. Take 4 oz of hops and 1 gallon of water and boil for 30 minutes. Strain, using 1 quart of this liquid combined with 1/2 gallon of molasses, 2-4 ounces essence of spruce and 4 gallons of warm water. Pour the mixture into a freshly cleaned cask and add yeast. Shake well and allow to stand for 10-14 days. Do not place bung in cask or the fermentation will blow it off.

Spruce beer was a common beverage of the British enlisted men at Fort Niagara and throughout North America. The drink was considered more healthy than spirits. Spruce beer, along with fresh fruits and vegetables, was also believed to be a preventative for scurvy. [7]

The lack of spruce beer at Fort Niagara during the winter of 1759-160 was considered to be a major factor in the death of 149 men from scurvy. Lieutenant Colonel Eyre reported to General Gage that he had "a Brewery going on here Upon a New Plan," but could not produce spruce beer for his scurvy ridden garrison due to a lack of molasses. Instead, hickory bark, maple syrup and sassafras were boiled together to "make a very agreeable Drink." This remedy was not considered to have been effective and was probably intended largely as a placebo for the men.

Spruce beer was also used at Niagara during the American Revolution. Major John Butler requested 54 items of stores on September 9, 1779, to resupply his rangers. Included in this list among frying pans, chocolate, blankets, cheese, and blacking balls, were "12 barrels Molasses, 10 boxes essence [of] spruce." [8]

•••••••

•••••••

Chocolate [9]
Officers' & Common Fare

1 oz unsweetened chocolate
1 quart milk
1 quart water
sugar
nutmeg or cinnamon

Grate chocolate finely and place in an open sauce pan with water. When chocolate is boiling, add milk and return to boiling. Allow to boil for 3 to 4 minutes, stirring carefully to avoid burning. Add sugar to taste.

•••••••••

Pork Chowder [11]
Common Fare

1 lb salt pork
1/2 lb dried peas
2 onions
2 lbs fish (whitefish, sturgeon, eel, bass were common)
1 Tbl flour

Soak dried peas overnight to soften. Mince pork and fish. Brown pork in kettle. Add fish, onions, peas and water to pork. Simmer for about one hour. Blend flour and a small amount to water into a paste and add to thicken the chowder. Season to taste.

•••••••••

Boiled Fish [13]
Common Fare

fish of your choice (whitefish, bass, sturgeon, herring)

Clean fish well. Remove all fins and scales, but leave the head. Boil in water until flesh falls from the bones. While boiling, it will be necessary to remove the scum which collects on the surface of the water. The fish should be cooked 5-10 minutes per pound. When done, season with salt and pepper to taste.

Fish Gravy [15]
Common Fare

1 Tbl butter
1 Tbl fat (lard) in which the fish was cooked
2 Tbl flour
1 cup boiling water
2 Tbl vinegar

Melt butter and fat in pot, add flour and blend until smooth. Add boiling water gradually, stirring until gravy thickens. Add vinegar and mix well.

· · · · · · · · ·

Three Grain Bread [17]
Common Fare

2 cups cornmeal
4 cups boiling water
2 tsp salt
2 Tbl dry yeast
1/2 cup water
1 tsp sugar
2 1/4 cups rye flour
2 cups whole wheat flour

First, make a "sponge" by pouring 4 cups of boiling water over the 2 cups of cornmeal and 2 teaspoons of salt in a large bowl. Stir and let stand until water absorbed and mixture is cool. Add yeast and 1 cup rye flour, stir to mix. Cover and allow to stand overnight in a cool place. The sponge will reman flat, but the yeast will have worked. Mix in the whole wheat flour and 1 cup rye flour, knead for 10 minutes on a board with 1/4 cup of rye flour on it. Set in a warm place to rise until doubled. Divide and shape into two 9-inch loaves placed on a well greased baking sheet or bread tins. Preheat oven to 375°. Bake for 45-50 minutes.

Patrick Campbell noted, in his Travel in North America, *that while at Niagara in 1792 he "crossed the river to the north side see the fishing, and saw 1008 caught at one hawl of a Seine net, mostly what is called here White fish, and a few Herring;...I saw several other kinds caught here, particularly the Sturgeon, which is a bad useless sort of fish, except for isinglass, of which it is said a deal might be made here."* [16]

Rice was a regular part of the British soldier's ration and was issued one day a week. The men of Fort Niagara's garrison obtained venison by trading with the Indians since they were not allowed to hunt. Turkey and bear were also brought to the fort by local Indians. These meats may be substituted for venison.[19]

Tin reflector ovens or "tin kitchens" were also used in this period of time, although we do not have any references to them being used at Fort Niagara. They were made of sheet tin. The "oven" would be placed next to the fire where it could reflect the heat within its interior, allowing food to cook more evenly. The reflector oven was popular for fowl or making baked goods such as tarts and cookies.[21]

Deer are plentiful in Western New York, and are still hunted, for food, in the region near Fort Niagara.

Soldiers of Niagara's garrison often traded with the local Indians for wild game such as deer and bear. Faunal remains in the Old fort Niagara archaeological collections suggest the use of many types of game in their diet. Common soldiers in the 1760's are known to have traded with the Indians for deer, bear and turkeys.[22] Wild turkeys are still found and hunted, for food, in the Western New York region near Fort Niagara.

Venison and Rice Stew [18]
Common Fare

4 lbs venison
1 large onion
2 1/2 quarts water
salt & pepper to taste
2 cups rice

Mince venison. Simmer venison and onion in water until meat is tender, about 3 1/2 hours. Add salt, pepper and rice. Cover pot and simmer for another 25-30 minutes or until the rice is tender. When done, most of the water should be absorbed.

• • • • • • • • •

Rack of Venison [20]
Officer's & Common Fare

6-8 lbs venison
1/2 to 1 lb salt pork

Tie salt pork to venison and place in roasting pan. Roast in reflector oven or over open fire (325º in oven) for 18 minutes per pound of venison. If salt pork is not available, baste the meat with butter throughout roasting time.

• • • • • • • • •

Roasted Turkey [23]
Officer's Fare

1 turkey (13-16 lbs)

Pluck feathers and clean turkey well, being sure to remove all organs. If means are available, stuff turkey loosely with a plain stuffing mixture (see Page 31). Spit turkey on a skewer (or place in a roasting pan for oven cooking). When spitted, tie up legs and wings of turkey to prevent falling off as turkey cooks. Roast turkey slowly (325º), being sure to turn bird every 20-25 minutes to ensure even cooking. Roast until steam comes from the breast of the bird. This should take approximately 2 1/2-3 hours.

Turkey Stuffing [24]
Officer's Fare

1 lb dried bread or crackers
1 lb raw salt pork
1 tsp sage
1/2 tsp summer savory
1/2 tsp pepper
salt to taste
1 egg

Crumble dried bread (crackers) very finely. Dice salt pork finely. Combine crumbs and salt pork. Add the seasonings to this and the egg. If the stuffing is dry, add 2 tablespoons of water to moisten. Stuffing should stick together, but not be wet to the touch. Place in cleaned bird or place in pot and bake at 350° for 30-45 minutes.

• • • • • • • • •

Passenger Pigeon Pie [26]
Officers' & Common Fare

6 pigeons (substitute cornish game hens)
1 Tbl butter
2 oz fat (salt pork or bacon strips)
1 1/2 Tbl flour
2 cups broth (chicken work well)
salt and pepper to taste
3 onions, sliced

Put the "pigeons" in a Dutch oven (or baking dish) with your fat (a strip of bacon is best, though less available to Niagara's soldiers). Place the oven or dish in a hot fire (450°) and bake for 5 minutes and take from fire. Meanwhile, melt 1 Tbl butter over low heat and stir in 1 1/2 Tbl flour. Slowly add broth and stir until smooth. Add onions and broth mixture to Dutch oven. Cover and allow to simmer for one hour over low fire (250°). Remove and debone the birds. Place in pie dish and add sauce. Cover with a pastry crust and bake in hot fire (450°) for 10-12 minutes or until crust is golden brown.

Old Fort Niagara's archeologists have found many turkey bones in their excavations.[25]

Passenger pigeons were a popular meal at Fort Niagara and through out early America, in part because of the ease of killing the birds. This eventually resulted in the extinction of the species. That is why Cornish hens are substituted in this recipe. The birds flocked in such numbers and were so docile that they could be netted or even clubbed to death. On February 12, 1760, Lieutenant Colonel Frederick Haldimand, then at Oswego, requested that "pigeon nets" be supplied to this garrison and that of Niagara. In 1773, Jabez Fisher, described "eating a hearty Supper of Pidgeons [sic] & Kildear [small shore birds]." Common soldiers would simply boil the tame birds without taking as much trouble as the above recipe. Elizabeth Simcoe, wife of Lieutenant Governor John Graves Simcoe of Upper Canada, wrote in 1795 that "Now the wild pidgeons are coming of which there is such numbers that besides those they roast & eat at present they salt the wings & breast of them in barrels & at any time they are food to eat after being cooked." [27]

A November 19, 1759, "return of Sheep Rum Vinigar Beef Tallow and Candles in Store at Niagara" listed 81 sheep. The presence of these animals at Fort Niagara is confirmed by the faunal remains of sheep recovered by Old Fort Niagara archeologists. [29]

Mutton Pie [28]
Officer's Fare

2 lbs mutton
2 cups flour
1/2 tsp salt
1/3 cup lard
1/4 cup water
1/4 cup chopped salt pork
2 eggs
1/2 cup flour

Soak mutton in water for 1 hour before cooking. Remove mutton, discard water and cut meat into cubes. Place in pot with 1 1/2 cups of water and simmer for 30 minutes. Meanwhile, mix up a pie crust. Measure 2 cups of flour and 1/2 tsp salt into bowl, cut in 1/3 cup lard and work until well-blended. Add 1/4 cup of water slowly, mixing as you add. Divide dough in half. Roll 1/2 of dough to fit baking dish. When mutton is cooked. Drain off water and save it. Place the cooked meat in the bottom of the dish, layered with salt pork. Beat eggs with a fork and combine with broth. Sprinkle 1/2 cup flour over the meat. Pour broth over the top and cover with remaining crust. Bake in a Dutch oven (or oven heated to 350º) until crust is golden brown.

Cook's Note: Whenever baking any pie, meat or fruit, it is best to start the pie baking in a hot oven-450º for about 10 minutes and then lower the heat to 350º for the remaining time. This gives you a nice golden brown crust without over cooking. When using the Dutch oven, put it directly in the hot coals for approximately 10 minutes, then pull out and put on hearth with coals banked under and on top of the lids as usual in Dutch oven cooking.

• • • • • • • • •

Rosewater [30]

Rosewater is made by placing the petals of fragrant roses in a jar and covering with French brandy. Tightly seal the jar and allow to stand for three to four days. Drain and strain the brandy into a bottle and cork it well. Vodka, a more modern alcohol, may be used in place of the brandy. Rosewater may also be purchased in specialty stores and the like.

Rosewater Currant Cake [31]
Officers' Fare

1 cup soft butter
1 1/2 cups sugar
5 eggs
2 cups flour
2 Tbl rosewater
1 tsp vanilla
3/4 dried currants or raisins

Cream butter and sugar together. Add eggs, one at a time, beating well each time. Mix flour in slowly, a little at a time. Add rosewater and vanilla and mix well. Fold in currants. Pour into a greased and floured baking pan. Bake (350º) for 30-40 minutes or until done.

• • • • • • • • •

Indian Potatoes [32]
Common Fare

1 1/2 lbs Indian potatoes ("Jerusalem artichokes")
1 gill (1/2 cup) butter
1 lemon
1/2 tsp salt
parsley

Peel Jerusalem artichokes and cook in boiling, salted water until tender. Test for tenderness after about 15 minutes. Artichokes should not be overcooked. Drain thoroughly and dress with a mixture of butter, lemon juice (about 3 tablespoons), salt and chopped parsley.

"Indian potatoes", known as Jerusalem artichokes today, were among the wild plants commonly gathered by the British soldiers at Fort Niagara. Such foraging could be hazardous, however. In October, 1767, a soldier returned to his barracks with roots he thought to be Indian potatoes. He boiled and shared them with his messmates. Within an hour, two of the men were dead and third died two days later. The unfortunate soldier had fatally mistaken "thapsia" or "deadly carrot" for Indian potatoes.[33]

The Jerusalem artichoke was first seen by Samuel de Champlain in 1605 in the gardens of the Indians on Cape Cod. To Champlain it tasted like the globe artichoke, and so called it an artichoke. Actually, the Jerusalem artichoke is a tuber-bearing type of sunflower. It is a knobby vegetable and ranges in color from purple to yellowish white; the flesh is while and crisp. The word Jerusalem is thought to be a corruption of "girasol," meaning, "turning to the sun." [35]

A "pommate" (possibly from pomace:, or "something crushed to a pulpy mass") of parsnips was part of a dinner served to British officers at Quebec in 1759. Parsnips were grown in Fort Niagara's gardens. They were popular because they could survive colder weather. Amelia Simmon's "American Cookery" notes that "they are richer flavored when plowed out of the ground in April, having stood out during the winter." Parsnips served as a good source of vitamins in the spring, when vegetables were scarce. [37]

Jerusalem Artichoke Relish [34]
Officers' Fare

1 lb Jerusalem artichokes
1 cup sugar
1 cup vinegar
8 whole cloves
1-2 sticks cinnamon
1/4 tsp salt

Wash and slice artichokes. Cook, covered, in a small amount of boiling salted water until tender about 10 to 15 minutes. Drain well. Heat sugar, vinegar, spices, salt and 1 cup of water till boiling. Pour over artichokes and refrigerate overnight.

• • • • • • • • •

A Pomate of Parsnips [36]
Officers' Fare

2 lbs parsnips
3/4 cup heavy cream
6 Tbl butter
2 Tbl brown sugar
1 Tbl lemon juice

Peel parsnips and cut into small pieces. Add the salt and parsnips to a pot of water and cook until soft - about 20 minutes. Mash parsnips and combine with cream, butter, brown sugar and lemon juice. Simmer while stirring often until well blended. Serve on fried or toasted bread.

Braided Fruit Bread [38]
Officers' Fare

1 pkg dry yeast
1 Tbl sugar
Let stand for 10 minutes un 1/2 cup of lukewarm water

Mix in:
1 egg
1/2 cup melted lard (cooled to luke warm)
2 cups lukewarm water
1 1/2 tsp salt
1/2 cup sugar

Add:
8 cups flour

Knead dough for about 10 minutes. Place in a greased bowl, cover and let rise for about 45 minutes. Punch down and divide into three parts. Roll each into an oval about 12 inches long.

Filling:
any fresh fruit (chopped if necessary)
sugar
suitable spices

Place fruit in center, sprinkled with sugar (1/4 cup or so) and desired spice. Cut strips an inch and a half wide along the sides of each oval. Fold strips alternating one side then the other to give it a braided appearance. Bake on ungreased sheets in the Dutch oven (or oven at 450º for 10 minutes then 375º for 25-30 minutes) until golden brown.

Cooks' Note:
Some nice combinations of spices are:
• peaches: nutmeg or cloves
• pears: cloves or cinnamon
• apples: cinnamon and nutmeg
• raspberries: cinnamon
• cherries: cinnamon or nutmeg
Be creative – mix your fruits and/ or spices.

John Graham was a Scottish surgeon for the 60th Regiment of Foot who lived with his family at Fort Niagara from 1768 until 1772. On December 1767, while still in Montreal he writes to John Davidson in Scotland to say that at their last assembly they had "Tea and Coffee, sweet Bread, Negris Port, and Claret." [39]

Seed Cake [40]
Officers' Fare

6 cups flour
2 cups sugar
8 eggs (beaten)
2 Tbl of caraway seeds
2 tsp yeast
2 tsp milk
2 tsp water

Heat water and milk together until lukewarm-add yeast and set aside for about 10 minutes. Mix sugar and eggs together and then stir in yeast mixture. Stir in flour and and caraway seeds. Bake in a well-greased hoop pan (springform pan) at 350º for approximately 45-55 minutes.

• • • • • • • • •

Peach Pie [42]
Officers' Fare

15 peaches or so
1 egg
2 Tbl flour
2/3 cup brown sugar
1/3 cup butter, softened
1/2 tsp cinnamon
1/2 tsp nutmeg

Peel, pit and slice peaches. Fill pie crust with sliced peaches. Combine egg, flour, sugar, and butter. Spread on top of peaches. Sprinkle lightly with cinnamon and nutmeg. Cover with top crust and seal edges. Pierce crust with fork. Bake (450 for 10 minutes and 350º for 25-30 minutes longer) until golden brown.

Apple Dumplings [44]
Officers' Fare

2 1/4 cups flour
1/2 tsp salt
2/3 cup shortening
6-8 Tbl cold water
6 baking apples, peeled and cored
6 Tbl brown sugar
1/2 tsp cinnamon
1/2 tsp nutmeg
6 Tbl butter
3/4 cup maple or maple-flavored syrup

Mix together flour and salt. Cut in shortening until resembles course crumbs. Add water, 1 Tbl at a time, mixing until moistened. Form into a ball and roll out a 18 X 12 inch rectangle on a well floured board. Cut into 6 six inch squares. Mix together sugar and spices. Place an apple on each pastry square and fill the centers with the sugar mixture divided into six parts (a heaping spoonful). Divide butter into 6 parts and place one on top of each apple. Moisten edges of pastry and pull up to wrap each apple, pinching dough together. Place dumplings in an ungreased 11 X 7 1/2 x 1 1/2 inch baking pan and bake at 450º for 15 minutes. Reduce heat to 350º, baste with maple syrup and continue baking for about 30 minutes until done. Keep basting every 10-15 minutes or so.

One apple dish which the English prepare is as follows:

"take an apple and pare it, make a dough of water, flour and butter. Roll it thin and enclose apple in it. This is then bound in a clean linen cloth, put in a pot and boiled. When done it is taken out, placed on a table and served. While it is still warm, the crust is cut on one side. Thereupon they mix butter and sugar, which is added to the apples; then the dish is ready. They call this apple dumplings, sometimes apple pudding." [45]

Apple Pan Dowdy
Officers' Fare

Apple Pan Dowdy gets it name because traditionally before it is served-one "dowdies" it or breaks up the crust with a spoon or knife and mixes the crust in with the apple mixture consequently, over the years, this type of "mixed up" appearance has been applied more to people than desserts. It is common in our language for an individual to be "dowdy" in appearance. [46]

2 cups soft bread crumbs
1/4 cup butter, melted
1/2 cup sugar
1/2 tsp cinnamon
1/2 nutmeg
dash of salt
10 cups thinly sliced apples (peeled if desired)

Syrup:
2 cups brown sugar & 1 cup water boiled gently for five minutes
or 1/2 cup molasses, 1/4 cup water & 3 Tbl melted butter
or 1 cup maple syrup

Sauté the bread crumbs in 1/4 cup butter. Mix apples with sugar, nutmeg, cinnamon and salt. Put apple mixture in large greased baking dish, pour syrup over the apples and place buttered bread crumbs on top. Bake in Dutch oven (oven at 350º) for 30-40 minutes, until apples are soft. Remove from the oven. "Dowdy" the crust by gently breaking it up and stirring. Return to the oven for 10 minutes longer.

Cook's Note: This recipe can also be made with a double pie crust which you roll out on a 15X 11 inch rectangle, brush with melted butter, fold in half, brush with more butter, fold again and seal the edges. Begin the process all over again by rolling the crust back out to the 15 x11 inch rectangle-brushing with butter again and folding. Chill the pastry. Roll it back out to 15 x 11 rectangle and place on top of the apple mixture which has been put into a 9 x 13 inch baking pan. Turn edges over and flute. Bake at 450º for 10 minutes and then turn down oven and continue baking at 350º for 30 minutes more. Remove from oven and "dowdy" the crust . Return to the oven for 10 minutes more.

Whipt Syllabub [47]
Officers' & Common Fare

1 pint cream
1 cup dry white wine or sack
1 lemon
3 egg whites
sugar
nutmeg

Combine cream, wine and egg whites. Add sugar to taste, about 1 tablespoon. Grate in nutmeg and the skin of the lemon (grated lemon peel). Using a whisk, whip ingredients until they froth. Skim and discard froth. Pour into glasses to serve.

Cooks' Note:
Here is another version which does not use raw, uncooked egg:
1 cup dry white wine
1/4 cup sugar
1/4 cup brandy
1 lemon
2 cups whipping cream

Mix the wine, sugar and brandy together. Let this stand until sugar dissolved. Meanwhile, grate the lemon to get 1 tablespoon of grated lemon zest and then squeeze for 1 tablespoon of lemon juice. Add to wine mixture. Add cream, and whip till soft and fluffy. Pour into dessert glasses to serve.

• • • • • • • • •

Wine Syllabub [50]
Officers' & Common Fare

3 Tbl lemon juice
3/4 cup sugar
1 cup Madeira wine
1 pint heavy cream
cinnamon
nutmeg

Dissolve sugar in lemon juice and wine. Whip cream and carefully fold into liquid mixture. Add cinnamon and nutmeg to taste. Chill and serve.

The name syllabub comes from the wine used to make it (imported from Sillery, France, in colonial times) and from "bub" an Elizabethan word for a bubbly drink. [48]

Syllabub was a very popular refreshment at "entertainments". In 1773 Jabez Fisher visited Niagara where "the gentlemen of the Fort being here treated us with the greatest complaisance... Drank some sylllabub, bid Adieu."

The common soldier, lacking the financial means to purchase lemon and sack or wine, would instead use cider and milk, adding cream over the top of his syllabub. [49]

This English favorite was carried by the soldiers to each new post. A hasty pudding was a common dessert, thick and sweet. Figuratively, a wet, muddy road might have been described as "quite a hasty pudding" during the eighteenth century. [51]

Hasty Pudding [51]
Common Fare

4 1/4 cups water
1 cup oatmeal
1/2 tsp salt
Milk or cream
Butter
Sugar, molasses, maple syrup or honey for sweetening.

Bring a quart of water to a boil in a pot. Remove from the fire. In a separate container, mix 1/4 cup of water and 3 Tbl oatmeal together. Add the oatmeal mixture and salt to the pot of water. Place on fire again. Slowly add the remaining oatmeal-1/4 cup at a time, stir to blend and bring pot back to a boil before adding the next gill. This should take about half an hour. Serve hot with milk or cream, butter and sugar, molasses, maple syrup or honey to taste

Cook's Note: Cornmeal (Indian Meal) or rye may replace the oatmeal. With unused mush, you may chill, slice and dust with flour to fry in butter or lard. Serve with your choice of syrup or honey.

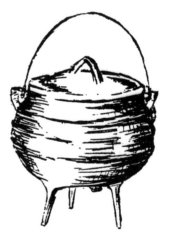

Hot Buttered Rum [53]
Officers' & Common Fare

2 gallons cider
1 pint maple syrup
1/2 lb butter
2 quarts dark rum

Mix cider and syrup. Bring to boil. Add butter and remove from the fire. Add rum and serve. Do not allow to reboil. Makes about 50 six-ounce servings.

• Another version for a spicy, single serving is:
1 Tbl sugar
1 jigger dark rum
1/4 tsp cinnamon
1 cup hot cider
1 tsp butter
fresh grated nutmeg

Mix sugar and 2 tablespoons of hot cider in a mug. Add butter, rum and cinnamon. Stir and fill with the rest of the hot cider. Sprinkle with nutmeg.

• Yet another version which serves four:
1 cup water
1/2 cup honey
1 1/3 cups dark rum, warmed
2 Tbl butter
Fresh grated nutmeg

In saucepan heat water and honey until boiling; stir in warm rum. Pour into serving mugs. Top each with a pat of butter and a sprinkle of nutmeg.

Cook's Note: If you have never tried grating your own nutmeg, we strongly encourage you to do so. Buy a small grater and whole nutmeg from the spice aisle. Fresh grated nutmeg is very easy to do and the flavor is outstanding. You may never buy ground nutmeg again.

• BRITISH OCCUPATION •
Revolutionary War & Holdover Period 1775-1796

The years of the American Revolution were very busy at Fort Niagara. The companies of the Eighth (King's) Regiment of Foot, and a small Royal Artillery detachment were reinforced by other regular units and large numbers of Loyalists and Native American allies. It became quite difficult to provide the quantities of provisions necessary.

When war broke out in 1775, Lieutenant Colonel John Caldwell was faced with providing provisions for the Indian councils held there. One of his most important duties was to maintain the Indians' friendship for the British Crown. To do so was costly to the garrison's foodstocks since the King's guests had to be well-fed. In the spring and summer of 1775 there were even greater problems because of the rebel moves against Quebec to block the movement of supplies. Fort Niagara , the headquarters for the upper lake posts, was expected to provide for the provision needs of these satellite stations.

To make matters worse, the rations were substandard. Contractors sold flour which was old, musty and sour-the oatmeal being the same way. Transporting provisions to Niagara left the boatmen up to their old tricks of letting out the brine to lighten to load and then refilling the barrels of salt pork with fresh water which would cause it to rot after sitting.

In 1779, the worst crisis was to come to Niagara. The supply fleet to Canada only contained about half of the quantity of provisions ordered. Rebel privateers captured four vessels loaded with foodstuffs. Fort Niagara was to become a haven for the Iroquois. The Six Nations were to be punished for their allegiance to the King and their raids from Niagara on the farms of New York and Pennsylvania. The Continental Army, under the direction of General John Sullivan was to attack them. Not only were the Iroquois villages destroyed but their corn crops were plundered. With their food supplies destroyed, the Six Nations had little choice but to gather at Niagara and rely on British support. Loyalists were also forced to flee to Niagara as well. With an additional 5000 people to rely on the storehouses at Niagara-numbers of them died from malnutrition as a result. That summer, the Royal Artillery detachment had been sent off to Detroit. In their place, a very small contingent of Hesse Hanau artillerists (Germans) were sent down from Quebec to take their place.

The officers of Fort Niagara sent large parties of Iroquois and Loyalist rangers (Butler's Rangers were the main attachment here) to wage a violent campaign against New York's Mohawk Valley and the Pennsylvania farming settlements. Requests for provisions while out in the field contained many interesting items of food. On September 9, 1779 , Butler requested:

> *4 [boxes] chocolate, 300 lbs. Coffee, 700 lbs. Bohea Tea, 200 lbs Green do [Tea],*
> *30 Barrels Brown Sugar, 3000 lbs. Loaf sugar, 60 lbs. Pepper, 3000 lbs. Cheese,*
> *90 lbs. Mustard, 100 gallons Vinegar, 12 Barrels Molasses, 10 Boxes essence [of]*
> *spruce.*

In 1781 a number of Loyalist settlers began farming at Niagara, mainly on the west side of the river (now known as Niagara-on-the-Lake, Ontario). This marked the true beginning of the settlement at Niagara. Some of the Butler's Rangers became farmers and by 1782 large quantities of vegetables and root crops provided the garrison with its need, even in winter. [1]

All of this brought more variety to the types of foods that could have been prepared and eaten at Fort Niagara. Included in this section are not only British, but, German and Native American recipes common to this period of time.

Ration Stew [2]
Common Fare

1 lb salt pork
1/2 lb dried peas and/or rice
fresh or dried vegetables according to the season

The ingredients and instructions for British Ration Stew of this time frame (1775-1796) at Fort Niagara are the same as 1759-1775. Please see Page 27, in the "British Occupation, 1759-1775" section.

• • • • • • • • •

Tea
Officers' Fare

loose tea
water

Place 1 cup water for every cup of tea you wish to make into a kettle and bring to a boil. Meanwhile warm a teapot by filling it with very hot water. When kettle is boiling, pour water out of teapot and measure 1 teaspoon tea per cup of tea desired into teapot. Add boiling water. Allow to steep for 5 minutes. Pour into cups using a strainer to catch loose leaves.

Cook's Note: Herbal teas were also used for medicinal purposes at this period of time. The following herbal teas are listed as commonly used among Native American populations.[5] These all grow in the area and might have been used here:
•Acorn shells were roasted and steeped; •Bergamot (bee balm or oswego tea) leaves-sore throats and upset stomachs; •Blackberry leaves-relieve diarrhea; •Borage leaves and flowers were made into a tonic to cure a cough; •Chickory leaves and blossoms were steeped to relieve mucus congestion; •Clover leaves and blossoms were used as a diuretic to cure urinary tract infections; •Comfrey leaves and roots provided internal and external healing; •Goldenrod leaves and flowers reduce phlegm; •Mint leaves make a beverage to soothe the stomach; •Rose hips, high in Vitamin C, prevented scurvy; •Sassafras leaves, roots and bark reduced fevers and acted as a spring tonic; •Sumac berries relieved kidney infections; •Witch Hazel leaves were dried and used for burns and insect bites.

The ration for the British soldier was one pound of bread or flour, one pound of salt pork, one-half pound of rice on the seventh day. The ration was supplemented with one ounce of butter daily. Women who were married to the soldiers received one-half ration and their children a quarter ration. Officers received multiples of the daily ration according to their rank which allowed them to support families or servants. [3]

The Hessians had a difficult time getting used to the salted meat as was noted by Johann Conrad Döhal in his diary in July of 1777. [4]

Prior to the time of the American Revolution, tea was a more popular drink in America than coffee. Early in the century, the ability to buy tea was a status symbol, but, by the middle of the 1700's. Tea, in numerous varieties, was available to most colonists. Tea was on the list of supplies requested from Fort Niagara for the use of Butler's Rangers in 1779. Mrs. Simcoe recorded a 1795 visit to the home of Adam Green who lived near Burlington Bay at the western end of Lake Ontario. They treated his daughter, who was sick with consumption, with a tea made of Sarsaparilla. [6]

Plain Cake [7]
Officers' Fare

6 eggs (4 large eggs)	1 lb flour (3 1/2 cups)
1 lb butter	spices (as available)
3/4 lb sugar (1 1/2 cups)	

Optional: 1 gill of rosewater or 1 gill of wine
        (1 gill=4 fl. oz)

Allow butter to stand to room temperature until soft. Cream together butter, sugar and eggs. Add flour slowly, blending well. Spices may be added as you wish. Turn into a greased baking pan. (9 x13) Bake at 350º for 35 minutes, or until done.

• • • • • • • • •

Apple Pie [9]
Officers' Fare

4-5 apples
1/2 cup brown sugar
1/2 tsp cinnamon
1/2 tsp nutmeg
1 Tbl butter
1 Tbl rosewater
1 pie crust

Peel and core apples. Cut into slices. Fill pie shell (see Page 47) with apple slices. Sprinkle with sugar, spices and rosewater. Dot with butter. Cover with top crust and seal edges. Pierce top crust with fork, glaze with milk and sprinkle with sugar. Bake in moderate oven (350º) for 35-40 minutes or until crust is golden brown and the apples have sauced.

Pie Crust [10]
Officers' & Common Fare

2 1/2 cups flour
3/4 cup lard
4-5 Tbl cold water
1/4 tsp salt

Rub lard and salt into the flour thoroughly until a hand-ful of it clasped tightly will remain in a ball. Wet it with cold water. Roll dough onto a board. Rub over the surface of dough and board with flour. Use just enough to keep dough from sticking. Roll dough lightly and quickly. Always roll away from you. Place crust in a pan and set aside in cool place until filling is ready.

• • • • • • • • •

Rusks [11]
Officers' Fare

1/4 lb butter, melted
1 cup milk
7 eggs
6 Tbl sugar
1 package dry yeast
3 cups rye flour
3 cups whole wheat flour

Beat the eggs in a mixing bowl. Add 1/2 cup milk, and 1/4 lb melted butter. Add yeast, sugar and 3 cups flour. Stir for 2 to 3 minutes. Allow to rise for 1/2 hour in a warm place. Add remaining 3 cups flour and work it in well-stiff, but not too stiff. Divide into about 2 dozen cakes each about 3-4 inches in diameter and flattened. Fry on a heavy greased skillet for about 7 minutes. Watch to avoid burning. Flip and press down, cook 7 minutes and serve hot with butter.

While on a journey to Fort Niagara, Robert Hunter, Jr., a young London merchant, enjoyed rusks at breakfast on a number of occasions such as Sunday, July 3, 1785, "We breakfasted very heartily at seven o'clock this morning on cold beef, rusks and butter, and wine and water. It did me an amazing deal of good." he recorded in his diary. [12]

Mrs. Elizabeth Simcoe's diary for July 2, 1783, records, "we treated them with Cherries. The Indians are particularly fond of fruit. We have 30 large May Duke Cherry trees behind the house & 3 standard Peach trees which supplyed us last autumn for Tarts & Deserts during 6 weeks besides the numbers the young men ate." [14]

Tarts [13]
Officers' Fare

2 eggs
1/2 cup cold water
3/4 lb butter, softened
1 lb flour
fresh fruit (or dried fruit, out of season)
sugar
nutmeg, cloves, cinnamon, allspice

To make the pastry, separate egg yolks from whites and set aside. Whip egg whites until frothy, but not stiff. Add to the whites, 1/2 cup cold water and 1 egg yolk. Blend together until it forms a smooth paste. In another bowl mix flour and butter until smooth. Slowly combine egg mixture with flour mixture, one-half cup at a time, blending thoroughly each time until it forms a dough. Roll on well floured surface until one-quarter inch thick and cut into four inch squares. Set aside. Make filling by peeling & pitting(if necessary), chopping, and cooking fruit until soft and thick. Sweeten to taste and blend in desired spice(s). Using left over egg yolk, if desired, beat with a fork and add about 1 tablespoon of water. Place about one tablespoon of fruit mixture in center of pastry, fold over, brush with egg yolk mixture and bake (400 º) on a well greased cookie sheet for 8-10 minutes or until golden brown.

Cook's Note: Fruits suggested for filling, available at Fort Niagara in the eighteenth century were apples, blackberries, cherries, cranberries. currants, peaches, hurtleberries, may apples, pears, raspberries and strawberries.

Zwieback or German "Twice Baked" Bread
Officers' & Common Fare

1 cup milk	3/4 tsp salt
1/3 cup honey	1/2 tsp cardamom
2 tsp active dry yeast	2 Tbl oil
3 cups flour	

Scald the milk, stir in honey and oil, let cool until luke-warm. Add the yeast and let it sit for about 10 minutes. Stir together the flour, salt and cardamom. Add to the milk mixture and knead well in bowl. Cover and let rise in a warm place until double (about 45 minutes). Punch down and, if dough feels sticky, add more flour. Shape into loaf and place in a greased pan. Cover and let rise again. Bake at 400 º until golden for 30-35 minutes. Remove from the oven and let cool completely. Slice into 1/2 inch rounds and rebake in a 200º oven for 1 hour. Cool and store in tightly covered tins.

• • • • • • • • •

Bubble and Squeak [18]
Common Fare

2 cups left over beef, cut into bite-sized pieces
2 small head cabbage, chopped
1 Tbl vinegar
1 cup water
salt and pepper
butter

Cook cabbage in 1 cup of water until tender. Add beef, vinegar, salt, pepper and butter. Cook until warm.

As the Hessians lay anchor at Dordrecht, waiting to make the journey to America, it was noted that "The English ships provisions seem rather scant to us. They consisted of one pound of bread, zwieback,, and one-eighth of rum...each man received a half pound of salted beef or pork on Sunday, Tuesday, Thursday, and Saturday. The other days we received some butter and cheese. Other vegetables were peas, rice, and flour." Whereas in their journey on the Main Rhine Waal and Meuse rivers lacked nothing, including the daily ration of two pounds of bread and a pound of meat. They were also able to purchase sufficient vegetables, barley, rice, sauerkraut, cabbage and flour because they had a complete ship, fully loaded traveling with them. [15]

Sauerkraut [16]
Common Fare

20 lbs cabbage
1/2 lb coarse salt

Shred cabbage. Layer with salt in a large ceramic crock, starting with cabbage and ending with salt. Cover with a clean cloth. Weight it down with a plate and a large rock. Keep it below 60° and above 40°. Remove scum daily and replace with a clean cloth. Let it stand at least a month. It can be canned or frozen. Makes 8 quarts.

• • • • • • • • •

Pork with Cabbage
Common Fare

4 pork chops (in place of salt pork)
salt and pepper
1 Tbl fat
8 cups cabbage, coarsely chopped
1/3 cup onion, chopped
1 apple, pared and chopped
1/2 cup water
1/2 tsp savory
1/4 tsp salt
1/2 cup milk
1 Tbl flour

Season the chops with salt and pepper. Melt fat in Dutch oven; brown pork chops. Remove and set aside. Place pork chops back into oven and cover tightly. Bake at 350° in the oven for 40-45 minutes or until pork chops are well done. Remove pork from oven and keep warm. Stir together flour and milk. Add to cabbage mixture and place on stove top on medium high heat. Cook and stir until thick and bubbly. Return pork chops and serve.

The provisions brought to the Hessians after Burgoyne's defeat at Bennington brought about this comment from on German officer, "Pork at noon, pork at night, pork cold, pork warm. Friends, although with your green peas and crabs' tails you would have looked with loathing at our pork, yet pork was to us a lordly dish, without it which we should have starved." [17]

Colcannon [19]
Common Fare

6 green onions
2/3 cup milk
4 cups mashed potatoes
4 cups cabbage, chopped into bite-sized pieces and cooked
salt and pepper
2 Tbl butter, melted

Chop green onion and put into pan along with milk. Bring just to a boil, remove pan from heat and set aside. Mix cabbage and potatoes. Add salt and pepper.   Stir in milk and onions. Put into baking dish and spread melted butter on top. Bake in a 350° oven for 20 minutes, until the top is browned.

• • • • • • • • •

Kedgeree [20]
Common Fare

3 cups dried peas
1 1/2 cups rice
6 cups water
3/4 tsp ginger
salt and pepper
parsley
1 onion, cut into rings
1 egg, hard-boiled

Soak dried peas overnight. Drain water and add rice and the 6 cups of water. Cook for 2 hours. Add ginger, salt and pepper to taste. Cook 1 to 2 more hours. Kedgeree should have thick consistency. Fry onion in skillet until translucent. Slice egg into rings. Garnish with parsley, fried onion rings and hard-boiled egg slices.

This would be a simple but yet more imaginative way to use one's rations. In England it is a very popular breakfast dish with smoked fish, curry powder and raisins added. Lemon wedges are an added garnish for this.

Mrs. Elizabeth Simcoe related that her cook could also make "veal cutlets" out of fresh sturgeon. "Cook knows how to dress parts of them cutting away all that is oily & strong, make excellent dishes from Sturgeon such as mock turtle soup, Veal Cutlets & it is very good roasted with bread crumbs", she wrote in 1792. [22]

Wiener Schnitzel or Veal Cutlets [21]
Officer's Fare

1 1/2 lb veal (or cutlets)
3/4 cup dried bread crumbs
2 egg whites
1/4 cup butter or bacon fat

Slice veal into thin (1/4 inch) strips. Beat egg whites in a shallow bowl. Spread bread crumbs in another bowl. Dip each strip of veal into egg whites and then bread crumbs. Melt fat in a spider and fry meat for 3 to 4 minutes or until browned. Turn and fry other side.

• • • • • • • • •

Turtle Soup [23]
Common Fare

1 lb turtle meat, cut into 1/2 inch pieces
fat for frying
2 cups chopped cabbage
2 stalks of celery, chopped
2 carrots, chopped
1 onion, chopped
6 whole peppercorns
3 sprigs parsley
2 cloves garlic
2 bay leaves
1 1/2 tsp salt
1 cup thinly sliced mushrooms
1/2 cup dry sherry
Optional: modern convenience
1/4 tsp Kitchen Bouquet

Brown meat in a small amount of hot fat. Stir in 1 cup of water, cover and simmer until tender about 1 1/2 hours. Meanwhile simmer together the cabbage, celery, carrot, onion, peppercorns, parsley, garlic, bay leaves and salt with 5 cups water for 1 hour. Strain broth and discard vegetables and spices. Stir in undrained turtle meat, mushrooms and sherry. Heat through. Stir in Kitchen Bouquet and serve.

Pickled Beets
Officers' & Common Fare

4-5 medium beets
1 large onion, sliced or pearl onions
1/3 cup water
1/3 cup sugar
1/3 cup vinegar
1-2 cinnamon sticks

Cook beets until tender. Peel and slice into bowl or crock along with onions. Heat together water, sugar and vinegar until just boiling. Pour over beets and add cinnamon stick. Keep covered in cool place. They are better to eat if they sit for a couple of days first.

Cook's Note: These will keep for a long time in a refrigerator or may be canned. You can also use 2 cans sliced beets in place of the fresh ones you have to cook.

• • • • • • • • •

Gingerbread [24]
Officers' Fare

2 1/3 cups flour
1 cup molasses
1 tsp pearl ash (baking soda-see sidebar)
1/3 cup boiling water
1 tsp ginger
1/3 cup butter
1/2 tsp cinnamon

Combine flour, ginger, cinnamon and baking soda in a bowl. In a separate bowl, add molasses and butter to the boiling water. Stir into this the dry ingredients. Knead dough until it is stiff. Set aside in a cold place until dough is thoroughly chilled (approximately 15 minutes). Roll out dough on floured board. Bake in hot Dutch oven 350º for 15 minutes or in a tin kitchen for 10-12 minutes.

Baking sodas and powders were not discovered yet that is why there is a reference to wood ash. Until 1800, eggs or small amounts of yeast were added to cakes as a leavening agent. Pearl ash (potassium carbonate, was obtained by leaching the ashes of wood or other plants and then purifying them by heating and recrystallizing them. Salteratus or "aerated salt", sodium bicarbonate (baking soda) replaced pearl ash around 1830. Baking powder, the combination of two parts of soda with two parts of cream of tartar, was used soon after. Commercial baking powder was sold in the 1850s whereas the first pure baking soda as we know today was not produced until the 1870s. [25]

Flummery [26]
Common Fare

oatmeal
water

Mix the oatmeal into cold water and let it steep for a night and a day. Then pour it off clean and add as much more water; let it stand again for the same amount of time. Strain it through a very fine sieve and boil it until it is as thick as hasty pudding; stirring all the time. When first strained you may add 1 Tbl sugar and two of orange flower water. Or, simply place oatmeal and water in a kettle. Bring to a rolling boil until the oatmeal reaches a "jelly-like" state.

• • • • • • • • •

Shrub [28]
Officers' Fare

2 quarts brandy
juice of 5 lemons
peels of 2 lemons
1/2 whole nutmeg
3 pints white wine
1 1/2 lb sugar

Place brandy, lemon juice, peels and nutmeg into a large bottle. Let stand for 3 days. Add wine and sugar. Mix well and strain twice. Rebottle.

• • • • • • • • •

Mulled Cider [29]
Officers' & Common Fare

1 gallon cider
2 cups brown sugar
6 sticks of cinnamon
2 tsp whole cloves
2 tsp salt

Dissolve brown sugar into the cider. Bring to a boil. Add cinnamon, salt and cloves. Let simmer for 15 minutes. Strain to remove cloves. Serve hot.

Fruit Jam
Officers' Fare

Take any fruits you like or combinations of them. Combine an equal amount of fruit and sugar in a large saucepan and boil the mixture for 5-10 minutes until thick. Keep in a container with a cover in a cool place. Small crocks work well.

• • • • • • • • •

Scones [30]
Officers' Fare

2 cups flour
2 tsp cream of tartar
1 tsp baking soda
1/4 tsp salt
1/4 cup lard
1 egg, slightly beaten
1/3 cup milk

Mix flour, cream of tartar, soda and salt together. Cut in the lard until it resembles coarse crumbs. Add egg and milk until soft dough forms. Do not over mix. Knead dough on floured surface. Pat into circle 3/4 inch thick. Cut into circles with a glass or biscuit cutter or into triangles. Bake at 450° for approximately 10 minutes or until golden brown.

Cook's Note: These can also be fried at a low heat using a spider. Variations include:
• Sweet tea scones: Add 2 Tbl sugar and 1/2 cup raisins, cut into squares and sprinkle with sugar and cinnamon, fold in half and bake
• Cheese scones: Add 1 cup grated cheese
• Herb Scones: add 2 tsp fresh or 1 tsp dried herbs (chives, parsley, tarragon, rosemary, oregano, salted herbs, etc.)
• Jam scones: make basic dough. Roll into 2 circles. Spread the bottom circle with 2 Tbl jam. Brush edges with milk, place second circle on top and seal. Brush top with beaten egg and bake in Dutch oven.
• Treacle Scones: Add 2 Tbl molasses to milk before adding to flour. Add 1 cup chopped walnuts.
• Currant Scones: Add 1/4 cup currants to sweet dough.

The fruits that were available at Fort Niagara were apples, blackberries, cherries, cranberries, currants, peaches, hurtleberries, may apples, pears, raspberries and strawberries.

Queen Cakes [31]
Officers' Fare

2 cups sugar
1 lb butter
2 Tbl rosewater
8 eggs, separated
4 cups flour
2 cups dried currants
Optional: 1/4 tsp nutmeg, 1/4 tsp mace, 1/4 tsp cinnamon

Cream sugar and butter together and add rosewater. Beat egg whites until stiff and add to butter mixture. Beat yolks until light yellow and add to butter mixture. Gently mix in dry ingredients a little at a time and stir in currants. Fill greased little tins (muffin tins) 1/2 full and dust with sugar. Bake a 350º for 15-20 minutes or until golden brown.

• • • • • • • • •

Apple Butter
Officers' Fare

6 lbs apples
6 cups apple cider
3 cups sugar
2 tsp cinnamon
1/2 tsp cloves
1/2 tsp allspice

Core and cut the apples into pieces but do not pare them. In a large pot, cook the apples with the apple cider until the skins come away from the pulp. Put through a strainer to remove the skins. Put the pulp back into the pot and add sugar, cinnamon, cloves and allspice. Simmer on low heat, stirring frequently, until very thick. This may take a couple of days.
Cook's Note: After the pulp has been made and sugar and spices added to it-you may put it in a pan and bake it in a low oven or put it in a crockpot on low. Make sure you stir it every 15 minutes or so.

Apple butter is the one we most commonly associate with any type of fruit butter. However, it is very simple to make other fruit butters, simply by using the cooked pulp from any variety of fruit. You can even use the pulp that is left in the jelly bag after the juice has been extracted, when making jelly. Using fresh apricots, peaches, plums, prunes or grapes works especially well. When you are using fruits that are juicier than apples, crush them and add just enough water, not cider, to keep the fruit from sticking. Use spices according to your taste.

Bannocks or Oatcakes [32]
Officers' or Common Fare

1 cup quick-cooking rolled oats or 2/3 cup medium
oatmeal flour
2 Tbl flour
pinch of baking powder (woodash/pearl ash is traditional)
1/4 cup hot tap water
2 Tbl butter, melted
1/4 cup quick-cooking rolled oats

Put 1/2 cup oats into a blender-blend until fine powder.
Repeat with the second half cup. Combine oats, flour,
salt , baking powder into a bowl. Stir in hot water and
butter. Sprinkle a board with the remaining oatmeal; place
dough on the board.* Roll to a 10 inch circle; cut into 12
wedges. Place wedges on ungreased baking baking sheet.
Bake at 350º for 15 minutes. Turn off heat and open
oven door. Leave oatcakes in the oven till firm and crisp,
4-5 minutes. Serve warm with butter.

Cook's Note: * At this point you may knead the dough slightly. Roll
out into a 10 inch circle. Cut into wedges and cook on a warm
greased griddle until the edges curl.

• • • • • • • • •

Baked Johnnycakes [34]
Common Fare

2 cups water
1 cup Indian flour (yellow cornmeal)
1 Tbl butter
1/2 tsp salt

Mix water cornmeal, butter and salt. Cook and stir till
thickened. Cool. Shape into four 3-inch squares. Place
on greased baking sheet; make indentations in top of each
cake with the edge of a spoon. Bake at 400 º for 25
minutes. Serve with butter.

Johann Conrad Döhla, the Hessian, writes in his journal on November 8, 1781 that rations were very poor and they received no bread "except for an occasional uncooked Indian bread from the escort which was even worse than pumpernickel. And instead of bread, ... we received a little raw and half-cooked oatmeal, from which we occasionally baked bread pancakes." [33]

On October 29, 1781, Johann Conrad Döhla relates that they once again received "Indian flour, that is, flour made from Indian corn or grain, which we baked into bread on a fire of coals or hot ashes." [35]

Coffee was just as prevalent as tea during this period of time. On October 18, 1776, Captain George Pausch writes that everyone has received enough salted meat, zwieback and rum... However, on the officer's part, they are short of tea, coffee, wine and other cold drinks." [37]

British soldiers at Fort Niagara could expect eight ounces of rice per week, issued each Tuesday and Saturday in one-gill lots.

Sergeant Jabez Fitch, Jr., described that, as provisions ran low near Lake George, New York, in 1959, that he was forced to cook his rice without sweetening, butter or salt, that is tasted very good. Rice remained an item of issue at Fort Niagara until the British soldiers withdrew in 1796. United States troops continued to eat rice, but it was not a regular ration item. [38]

In his travels upon Lake Erie near Buffalo Creek in 1796, Isaac Weld, Jr., "found two farm houses, adjoining about thirty acres of cleared land. At one of these we procured a couple of sheep, some fowls, and a quantity of potatoes, to add to our store of provisions." Weld and his traveling companions had a meal prepared for them by the "old woman of the house," which consisted of coarse "cake bread, roasted potatoes, bear's flesh, salted, which last we found by no means unpalatable." The above recipe may indeed be used with "bear's flesh salted," but beef or other meats may be easier to obtain. [40]

Coffee [36]
Officers' Fare

2 oz fresh ground coffee
water
2-3 isinglass chips (optional)

Put coffee into a coffee pot and pour eight cups of boiling water on it. Let it boil six minutes, pour out a cupful two or three times, and return it again. Put 2-3 isinglass chips into it and pour one large spoonful of boiling water on it; boil it five minutes more, and set the pot by the fire to keep it hot for ten minutes.

Cook's Note: To "grind" coffee was to place the beans into a mortar and pound them with a pestle until they were the "grind" you desired. You can also "cook" whole coffee beans. In place of the isinglass chips, drop in one crushed eggshell and 1 egg white. Add 4 Tbl cold water (to settle grounds).

• • • • • • • • •

Rice
Common Fare

1 cup rice (brown long grain)
1 tsp salt
2 cups water
pepper and butter

Bring water to a boil, add rice and salt and cover tightly. Simmer until tender and water is absorbed, about 20-30 minutes. Season to taste with pepper and butter.

• • • • • • • • •

Roasted Potatoes [39]
Officers' & Common Fare

Potatoes (at least 1 per person you are serving)

Choose potatoes of about the same size. Wash thoroughly and peel. Place in boiling water for 10-15 minutes. Drain water and place under a roast of meat already mostly cooked. Baste with juice from the roast and cook potatoes 15-20 minutes on each side. Serve on platter with roast or in a separate bowl.

Potato Soup
Officers' & Common Fare

2-3 potatoes, pared and diced
1 large onion, chopped
1 tsp salt
pepper to taste
1 cup milk
2 Tbl butter

Cook potatoes and onion in about 4 cups water with salt and pepper. When potatoes are tender add 1 cup of milk and 2 Tbl butter. Heat until milk warm and butter melted. Do not boil.

• • • • • • • • •

Sallett (or Salad)
Officers' & Common Fare

scallions (green onions)
radishes
red and boston crunch lettuce
other assorted greens such as spinach, mustard greens, etc.
cabbage
cucumber

carrots, cooked
turnips, cooked
onions, cooked
beans, cooked
asparagus, cooked

vinegar
oil (olive or salad oil)
sugar
salt and pepper

Shred cabbage. Break up lettuce and other greens. Slice other vegetables including the cooked ones. Mix together. Sprinkle with salt, pepper and sugar. Mix oil and vinegar to taste and dress the salad.

Johann Conrad Döhla noted that the land in Staten Island in June 1777 was good and fertile where many crops are planted. "They also plant potatoes, which, however, are not as good as those we grow; they are watery because the ground is so rich. They also grow pumpkins, melons, beans, pickles, onions, apricots and other good garden produce in abundance. But plums such as in Germany are not grown here, only a different type of plum." [39]

Jabez Fisher, an adventurous Philadelphian traveling between the British forts in the Colony of New York during the summer of 1773, noted in his diary that "we went up to the Fort [Fort Ontario at Oswego], got some potatoes, sallad and milk." It could be likely that "sallett" was made at Fort Niagara because of the vegetable gardens which were there. [42]

The Native Americans considered the "Three Sisters" to be the most important foodstuffs. Corn, beans and squash were the "Three Sisters" which were planted together, one to help the other. This was done by forming hillocks, two to three feet apart and dropping the 4 corn seeds into each. Between the corn, rows of bean and squash were planted. The bean plants used the cornstalks for support and the squash spread out over the ground, shading it to keep the ground moist and choke out weeds.

Blackcaps (Blackberry Dumplings) [43]

3 cups blackberries (may also use blueberries)
1 cup sugar
3/4 cup water
1 Tbl butter

Dumplings:
1 cup flour
5 tsp baking powder
5 tsp sugar
1/2 tsp salt
1 egg
1/3 cup milk

In a pot, mix berries, sugar, water and butter. Bring to a boil, stirring often. Lower heat to simmer. Meanwhile, mix flour, baking powder, sugar and salt in a bowl. Stir together the egg and milk in another bowl. Mix wet and dry ingredients together until a soft dough forms. Drop by tablespoons into simmering berry mixture. Cover and simmer for 15-20 minutes. Serve warm with cream.

• • • • • • • • •

Baked Scraped Corn
(Ogoᵃ' sä' ohon' stä') [44]

corn on the cob

The green corn is scraped from the cob with a knife (or deer's jaw), pounded in a mortar or mashed in a wooden bowl with a stone, patted into cakes, sprinkled with dry meal and baked in small dishes. For baking in the ashes the cakes are wrapped in husk and covered with ashes. Embers are heaped over and a brisk fire built, this being kept going until the cakes were considered baked.

Corn Pudding [45]

1 dozen ears fresh sweet corn, husked (4 cups grated corn)
cream (evaporated milk)
4 eggs, lightly beaten
1 1/2 tsp salt
1/2 tsp pepper
2 Tbl sugar
6 Tbl melted butter

Use a sharp knife to slice of the tops of the kernels and
scrap the pulp into a bowl. Leave the scraped corn in a
colander so that the milk from the corn can drip into the
bowl. Measure enough liquid and add cream to make 1
cup. Combine with remaining ingredients and fold into
corn. Pour into baking dish or crock. Place on trivet in
Dutch oven and cover. Bake 1 hour or until set (knife
should come out clean when inserted into the center).

• • • • • • • • •

Popcorn Pudding
(Wataton' qwus odjis' kwa) [46]

Pop an amount of popping corn and then chop it.
Sprinkle the white meal with sugar and milk or cream.

• • • • • • • • •

Fried Cooked Green Beans
(None owi it is done) [48]

Green beans
Sunflower oil (or bear oil)
Salt

Cut green beans into 1 inch lengths and place into a
cooking pot. Cover with water and bring to a boil.
Simmer until just tender, remove from heat and drain. In
a frying pan, heat oil and add beans and fry. Salt to taste.

*The French as early as 1612 reported that the
Iroquois popped popcorn in a pottery vessel with
heated sand underneath and then used to make
popcorn soup.* [47]

Baked Squash *(Wandenyoᴰ soñduk)*[49]

Hubbard or other winter squash

Bake the squash in the ash of the fire. The Native Americans ate the whole squash, skin, seeds and all. You may also place the squash in a Dutch oven on a trivet and bake until tender. Cut in half, scoop out seeds and discard. Next scoop pulp into a bowl and discard skin. Season with salt, pepper and butter and mash together.

· · · · · · · · ·

Succotash *(Ogonᵃ' sä' ganon' dä)*[50]

2 cups lima beans, cooked	2 Tbl butter
2 cups corn, cooked	salt to taste

Mix ingredients together and warm in a kettle. Do not overcook.

· · · · · · · · ·

Fried Summer Squash *(Onya' sa')*[51]

2 crook neck squash, sliced thinly	salt & pepper
1 medium onion, slice thinly	butter

In a skillet, melt butter over a medium high heat. Add squash and onion. Fry until tender and golden brown. Season to taste.

· · · · · · · · ·

Indian Fried Bread (Ghost Bread)[52]

2 cups flour	1 cup milk
3 tsp baking powder	oil/ fat for frying
1/2 tsp salt	

Mix dry ingredients in bowl. Add milk slowly to biscuit consistency. Knead a few times on a floured board. Roll out or fit a 9 inch skillet with 1/4 to 1/2 cup of cooking oil, hot but not smoking. (Dough may also be cut into smaller pieces.) Roll dough to 1/2 inch thickness and put into skillet. Brown underside and turn over to brown other side. Serve with butter, jam, honey or maple syrup.

Indian Corn Soup (old recipe) [53]

4 qts. dry Indian corn kernels (commonly known as Tuscarora white corn)
1 qt hardwood ashes, sifted (oak, maple, beech, etc.)
1 lb dry red kidney beans, washed
3 lb salt pork, cut into small pieces

Put enough water in an old kettle to cover corn. Bring to a boil, add corn and ashes. Cook about 30 minutes, stirring frequently. This loosens the hulls on the corn. When hulls slip off the kernels by working between the fingers, drain, parboil, drain, rinse, and parboil again. Repeat several times until parboiled water looks clean and clear. Place it is a large kettle when kernels are clear and clean. Parboil washed beans separate until water is colored. Add both water and beans to corn. Add salt pork to corn and beans. Be sure to use plenty of water as corn swells while cooking. Cook 3 to 4 hours or until corn is tender, stirring occasionally and adding water as needed.

· · · · · · · · ·

Indian Corn Soup (modern recipe) [54]

1 large can hominy
1 small can red kidney beans
1-2 slices bacon, chopped

Stir together in a pot and simmer for one hour. Add salt and pepper to taste.

· · · · · · · · ·

Wild Onion Soup [55]

Wild onions, pulled with the "whiskers" cut off
Fresh or salt pork, chopped and fried
Water

Potatoes, cubed
Other vegetables such as string beans

Wash wild onions thoroughly. Chop into 1 inch pieces. Cook in water, add cooked meat and raw potatoes and other vegetables. Cook until vegetables are tender. Serve with Indian Fried Bread.

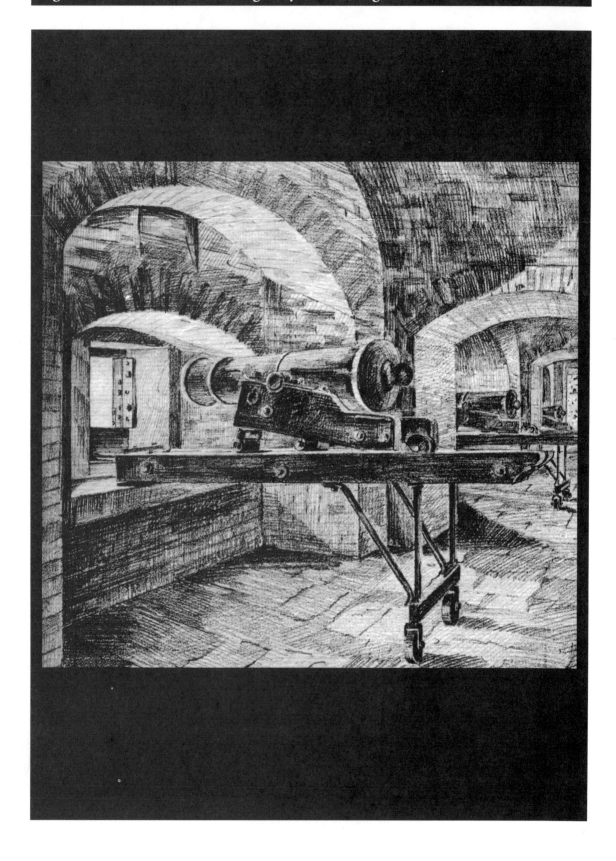

• The American Troops •
1796 – 1865

"Remember that beans, badly boiled, kill more than bullets; and fat is more fatal than powder. In cooking, more than in anything else in this world, always make haste slowly. One hour too much is vastly better than five minutes too little, with rare exception. A big fire scorches your soup, burns your face, and crisps your temper. Skim, simmer, and scour, are the true secrets of good cooking."

Captain James M. Sanderson, U.S. Commissary of Subsistence, "Camp Fires and Camp Cooking: or Culinary Hints for the Soldier" (1862, Government Printing Office, Washington).

On August 10, 1796, the United States troops took control of Fort Niagara. These men settled in to begin the dreary task of repairing the 70 year-old fort. It was difficult to supply Niagara as money and resources were in short supply. The quality of the flour was poor and it was delivered late. The daily ration specified in 1802 was "one and one quarter pound of beef or three quarter pound of pork, 18 ounces of bread or flour, a gill of liquor, salt, vinegar, soap and candles."[1] Fort Niagara was suddenly put in the position of being a border fortification with potentially hostile territory only six hundred feet away, the next closest American post at Oswego, 150 miles away. This new garrison was not only very isolated but its fortifications had been designed to guard against land attack. Now it was facing the wrong way.

Fort Niagara was only isolated for a short period of time as the lands on the New York side of the Niagara River were now surveyed and were rapidly being filled in with settlers. Youngstown, Lewiston, Manchester, Schlosser (the last two now part of the city of Niagara Falls), Black Rock, and Buffalo. As New York built towns and constructed new roads, the British were busy constructing a new fort across the river, Fort George. Relations between these two garrisons were friendly until June 1812 when the United States declared war on Great Britain.

Fort Niagara was unprepared for war, with its deteriorating fortifications and only 150 men, although Canada was also lacking men. Short of artillery, supplies and soldiers, Captain Nathan Leonard did what he could to improve his defenses. The New York Militia was also called into service at this time. In order to avoid friction between the militia and the regular army, the militia established a camp in Lewiston, six miles away.

Sadly, on the evening of December 18-19, 1813, the British gained entrance to Fort Niagara and after this surprise attack, were able to gain control. Partly in retaliation for the earlier bombardment of Fort George (May 25-26, 1813) and the burning of the adjacent town of Newark (present day Niagara-on-the-Lake) in the fall, the British burned Youngstown. Continuing up River Road, they were able to destroy Lewiston, Manchester, Schlosser, Black Rock and Buffalo by the end of the year. The Union Jack, flying over the post, was a powerful symbol – demonstrating that the British once again held this vital piece of United States territory. Following a seventeen month occupation, the Americans (under terms of the Treaty of Ghent) peacefully retook possession on May 22, 1815. The British moved back across the river to rebuild and repair, while life on the Niagara Frontier resumed, as burned villages and farms also rose from the ashes.[2]

During the 1820's the garrison at Niagara was to enjoy peaceful times. By 1821 regulations stated that bread would be placed on shelves and fresh meat was to be "hung out at the back windows on hooks-but not in the sun." A "mess" of soldiers (6-8 men) was to rotate the duty of cook with each to take his turn. This included musicians as well. The men were to use the "greatest care" in "scouring and washing the utensils employed in cooking." [3] However, with the construction of the Erie Canal in 1825, the Niagara region was basically put out of business. The Erie Canal note only ended nearly two hundred years of commercial traffic along the Niagara River but did way with the United States Army's chief reason for maintaining a post at the river's mouth. Troops were withdrawn and the the fort was put in the hands of a caretaker. In 1828 the fort was regarrisoned and did little more than routine duty until 1837 when a Canadian rebellion brought forth several incidents along the border This prompted action at Fort Niagara, which lay virtually in ruins. Between 1839 and 1841 the Army Corps of Engineers made extensive alterations and additions. The rebellion ended, easing border tensions and the post was once again abandoned.

Shortly after the outbreak of the War Between the States (1861) Fort Niagara was regarrisoned by the 7th United States Infantry. In 1863 the 7th Infantry departed leaving the fort ungarrisoned once more. However, new concerns that Great Britain might intervene on the side of the Confederacy, caused the United States to once again focus on the ancient fort. In the summer of 1863 new work was begun once more. By 1872, work was ceased and many of the new additions were left incomplete. [4]

• • • • • • • • • • • • • •

Recipes and rations: Following the War of 1812, the U.S. Army's ability to properly feed its troops came into question, and one small step in dealing with the concern showed itself in the form of vegetable gardens which were planted at most posts. The years leading up to the Civil

War saw numerous cook books printed in the private-sector, and many recipes from them were adapted for use by individual soldiers, military cooks, and civilian cooks-for-hire (employed by officers at some locations). Still, in spite of this, basic rations remined bland and were not very nutritional.

The American Civil War created an economic boon in the North. Generally speaking, the men in the Northern Army did have adequate amounts of food (unlike those in the South). During this time, canned goods started to appear. Condensed milk (invented by Gail Borden in 1856), and Van Camps pork & beans were among the products which found their way into the supply chain, although in limited numbers. In spite of this, the rations situation for the average soldier was anything but pleasant, and the age-old problem of diseases (such as scurvy and night blindness) caused by nutrient-deficient diets was a continuous concern. The daily allowance (on paper) for the Union soldier was supposed to be:

> *"twelve ounces of pork or bacon, or, one pound and four ounces of salt or fresh beef; one pound and six ounces of soft bread or flour or one pound of hard bread, or one pound and four ounces of corn meal; and to every one hundred rations, fifteen pounds of beans or peas, and ten pounds of rice or hominy; ten pounds of green coffee, or, eight pounds of roasted (or roasted and ground) coffee, or one pound of and eight ounces of tea; fifteen pounds of sugar; four quarts of vinegar;...three pounds and twelve ounces of salt; fours ounces of pepper; thirty pounds of potatoes, when practicable, and one quart of molasses."* [5]

Supplying fresh vegetables became a logistics nightmare, as they were quite heavy and bulky, and could not be transported easily and efficiently. In an atempt to deal with this matter, the War Department began testing a new, compressed, light-weight creation known as "desiccated vegetables." Composed of a mixture of dried cabbage, turnips, carrots, parsnips, potatoes, beets, peas, onions, beans, lentils, tomatoes and celery, the blend was formed into hard clumps designed to be soften and expanded when boiled. It did not go over well, and became affectionately known as "desecrated" vegetables. Supplying sufficient quantities of fresh meat and milk was an equally major problem. It would not be until the end of the nineteenth-century that some form of standardization of military recipes found its way into "official print," when, in 1896, the Commissary General of the U.S. Subsistence Department issued a manual for Army cooks, with each recipe written for "100" servings. Even then, it would be decades before a truly dependable system would find its way into the stomachs and hearts of those in uniform.

Article 27, Section 7, of the 1821 "General Regulations of the Army" notes of biscuit making that "in making biscuits of hard bread, the evaporation is about fifty-four pounds. So that the barrel of flour yields but one hundred and eighty-two pounds of biscuits." Niagara's American garrison was allowed to prepare either soft or hard bread. The hard bread was called "plain biscuit". This was made without milk or butter and produced a hard, cracker-like biscuit know to soldiers of a later generation as "hardtack". This recipe, drawn from Amelia Simmon's American Cookery, provides a more tasty, if somewhat less military dish.[7]

This ration soup was the standard fare for the common soldier of Fort Niagara before and during the War of 1812. He was told to add "hard or dry vegetables ... earlier than is above indicated." It was also noted that the meat (or part of it) could be taken out of the soup, but if this was done he was to add more water!

Plain Biscuit [6]
Officers' & Common Fare

2 cups flour
1 oz butter
1 egg
1/2 cup milk

Melt butter and add to the milk. To this add the egg and 1 cup of flour. Mix well. Continue to add the flour until a bread-like consistency is obtained. Knead until dough is soft. Break into sections and bake for 15-20 minutes at 350º. For more modern tastes, you might add 1/2 tsp baking powder to help the biscuits rise.

• • • • • • • • •

Ration Soup [8]
Common Fare

1 lb beef
5 pints water
vegetables of the season
salt
1/2 lb bread, sliced

Place 5 pints of water to 1 lb of beef in a pot and bring to a rolling boil, skimming off the foam as it cooks. Moderate the heat and add salt to taste. Add 1 pound of "vegetables of the season" such as peas, beans, carrots, potatoes, turnips, etc. Simmer for 1-2 hours. A few minutes before the end of simmering, add sliced bread. Reduce for 5-6 minutes. Add water to broth to replace losses before serving.

Salmon [9]
Officers' Fare

2-3 lbs salmon
3 Tbl butter
1 onion
1 stalk celery
1 carrot
1/2 cup vinegar
2 sprigs parsley
1 bay leaf
8 whole cloves
1/4 tsp pepper
1 quart water

Dice onion, celery, carrot. Melt butter in a spider (skillet). Add vegetables and sauté for 5 minutes. Add vinegar, water and spices. Bring to a boil. Let boil 5 minutes and then strain. Keep the liquid (broth) and discard the vegetables. Wrap the salmon in a piece of cheesecloth. Lay in the bottom of a kettle. Cover salmon with hot broth. Simmer uncovered for approximately 30 minutes. Remove fish from kettle. Uncover and remove the skin before serving. Serve garnished with egg sauce for a more elegant dish.

• • • • • • • • •

Egg Sauce [11]
Officers' Fare

4 Tbl butter
1 Tbl flour
2 hard-boiled eggs, diced
2 cups milk
1 Tbl lemon juice
salt and pepper

Melt butter over a low heat. Add the flour, stirring constantly, for 2-3 minutes. Heat milk separately. Add milk to butter and flour and stir. Cook about 3 minutes or until near a boil. Add lemon juice and diced eggs. Season to taste with salt and pepper.

Salmon was a commonly caught lake fish at Fort Niagara. Isaac Weld, Jr., in his published "Travels of 1795-97," mentioned that "Lake Ontario, and all the rivers which fall into it, abound with excellent salmon." Faunal remains from archeological explorations at Fort Niagara show that salmon was consumed here. A New England egg sauce is included to provide a "Yankee" flavor to this delicacy. Fort Niagara's commandants from 1800 through 1813, Major Moses Porter and Captain Nathaniel Leonard, were both natives of New England. Perhaps they enjoyed the Lake Ontario salmon with sauce from their home states. [10]

On January 6, 1813, Private Matthew Campbell was tried at Fort Niagara for "striking and cutting Catherine Brown with a knife." It seems that Campbell had used Catherine Brown's wash "kittle" to fry his meat in. When she removed it, he "sized holt of a knife, struck her in the arm and cut her." Catherine reported that "she got the kittle from some person in the yellow barracks and had it for the purpose of washing in." Campbell was convicted and sentenced to "10 cobbs and 2 weeks of hard labour." "Cobbing" was a beating on the behind. [12]

•••••••

"Beef and cabbage" has a long association with the U. S. army of the nineteenth century and is similar to the "bubble and squeak" of Niagara's earlier British garrison. As Late as 1862, when Captain James Sanderson published his Campfires and Camp Cooking; or Culinary Hints for the Soldier, *this recipe was included. Fresh beef was often available at Fort Niagara and this would have been a common meal. Drovers would come from Rochester, along the Ridge Road to Creek Road, with herds of cattle. A frequent last stop was Colonel Hathaway's tavern, located in Youngstown, which had cattle pens attached. This was located on the site of what is the present day "Ontario House."* [13]

Fry Meat
Common Fare

1 lb beef or 3/4 lb pork

Trim fat and save. Place fat into a pot and heat to "hissing hot". Cube meat into bite-sized pieces and add to pot. Fry for 12-15 minutes.

•••••••••

Beef and Cabbage
Common Fare

1 lb salt beef (or fresh beef)
2 medium heads of cabbage, shredded
salt and pepper
vegetables of the season (onions, carrots, potatoes, parsnips, etc.), diced

If using salt beef, soak it overnight in fresh water. Remove beef and discard water. Replace with cold water in a pot. Cook for three hours, skimming the foam off every 15 minutes or so. After 2 hours, add cabbage and vegetables to fill the pot. Boil gently for 90 minutes until vegetables are tender. Season to taste.

•••••••••

Green Peas [14]
Common Fare

1 gill (4 oz) dried peas
mint leaves
1 Tbl butter
1 tsp sugar
salt

Place peas in a pot, adding enough water to cover them, but no more. Add a couple of mint leaves, sugar and butter. Boil them until peas are tender. Drain and salt to taste.

Boiled Potatoes [15]
Common Fare

"To boil potatoes. Set them on a fire, unpared, in cold water, let them half boil, them throw some salt in, and a pint of cold water, and let them boil again till near done. Pour off the water, and put a clean cloth over them, and then the sauce pan cover, and set them by the fire to steam till ready."

• • • • • • • • •

Fried Potatoes [16]
Common Fare

4-6 medium potatoes
fat (shortening)
Optional: 1 onions, sliced

Slice raw potatoes and put into cold water to keep from turning brown. In a frying pan, heat fat until "hissing hot". Drain potatoes well and add with onions to pan. Fry until golden brown.

• • • • • • • • •

Brandied Peaches [17]
Officers' Fare

1 lb. sliced peaches
1/2 cup sugar
brandy to cover

Stir the brandy and sugar together in a saucepan. Add sliced peaches and simmer gently but do not boil. Remove from the heat, place in bowl to cool.

Alcoholism was a common problem in armies of the eighteenth and early nineteenth centuries. The pervasiveness of liquor is obvious from official documents and court martial records of the time. One garrison order from Fort Niagara dated October 12, 1813, stated that "in future no spirit of any kind, either rum, brandy, whiskey, wine, cider, will be permitted to be sold, bartered or in any way bargained for within this garrison on the bottom or within 100 yards of the barrier gate. No person will be permitted to pass in side the barrier gate with a pail, bucket, campkettle, tin pail, or canteen or any kind of cup that can contain spirits without a written permission from the commanding officer." This order, like many before and after, was often ignored by the common soldier (or officer). The problem was compounded by the fact that whiskey was a ration item in the United States service. [18]

• • • • • • •

Hardtack, pilot bread, hardbread – whether you be from the North or the South – was a staple for men on the march during the War Between the States. It was often accompanied by beef jerky. Alternately known as "tooth-dullers," "sheet iron," "crown breakers," or "worm castles." Hardtack was more something to be sucked on than chewed. In order to bite down on it it was often broken to smaller pieces. Dipped in hot coffee, it was more edible. Hardtack, the celebrated Civil War edible (or is it?) is referred ...

> *"I will speak of the rations more in detail, beginning with hard bread, or to use the name by which it was known in the Army of the Potomac, Hardtack. What is hardtack? It was a plain flour and water biscuit."* [22]

It got its name of "worm castles" because after being carried in hot, humid weather, it not only absorbed the moisture from the humidity but also from the sweat of the men carrying it.

This would make it easy to become inhabited–so the men often boiled it in their coffee to make the worms rise to the surface where they could be skimmed off the liquid. Another type of hardtack known as "skillygalee" was made by soaking the hardtack in cold water and then browning it in pork fat and seasoning to taste. [23]

Hot Buttered Toddy [19]
Officers' Fare

1 cup water
1/2 cup honey
1 1/2 cups dark rum, warmed
2 Tbl butter
Dash ground nutmeg

In saucepan heat water and honey till boiling; stir in warm rum. Top with butter and sprinkle with nutmeg. Makes 4 (6 oz) servings.

• • • • • • • • •

Hardtack (Hard Bread, Army) [21]
Common Fare

(Version 1)
Use one part of water and six parts of flour. Mix and knead. Roll the dough flat and cut into cracker shapes. Bake 20-25 minutes and cool off until completely dry before storing. The crackers should be as hard as bricks.

(Version 2)
Using a fork to mix the following ingredients well:
4 cups flour (preferably not white)
2 Tbl fat
2 Tbl cream of tartar
Dissolve in 1 c. water:
1 tsp of salteras (baking soda)
1 1/2 tsp salt

Combine all ingredients mixing well. Roll out the dough 3/8" thick with a rolling pin. Cut into 3" x 3" squares. Use a toothpick to put 16 holes (4 x 4 pattern) on each cracker. Bake 20-25 minutes at 450º. When done, let air-dry for at least 24 hours before you put in a bag or sealed container. Yield-11 or so crackers.

For all of the tales and jokes told of Hardtack, it should be noted that the United States Army did have regulations concerning it production. Hardtack for the Union Army was commercially produced by bakeries contracted with for that purpose, and came with its own set of guidelines and military-specific instructions. The following is from the 1863 specifications written by Lt. Col. C.L. Kilburn, Assistant Commissary General of Subsistence:

Hard Bread

Should be made of best quality of superfine, or what is usually known as extra superfine flour; or better, of extra and extra superfine, (half and half). Hard bread should be white, crisp, light and exhibit a flaky appearance when broken. If tough, solid and compact, is evident the fault is either in the stock, manufacture or baking; it should not present the appearance of dried paste. If tough and pasty, it is probably manufacture from grown wheat, or Spring wheat of an inferior kind. In all cases it should be thoroughly cooled and dried before packing. Kiln drying, where practicable, for long voyages, is particularly desirable; but if really and thoroughly dried in the oven, hard bread will keep just as well and its flavor is not destroyed. To make good hard bread, it is essential to employ steam; hand work will not do.

The dough should be mixed as dry as possible; this is, in fact, very essential, and too much stress can not be placed on it. Good stock, dry mixed, and thoroughly baked, (not dried or scalded) will necessarily give good hard bread. If salt is to be used, it should be mixed with the water used to mix the dough. Both salt and water should be clean. Bread put up with the preceding requirements should keep a year; but as a usual thing, our best bread as now made for army use, will keep only about three months. Good, bread, packed closely and compactly should not weigh, net, per barrel, more than 70 or 80 pounds; should it be heavier that 80 it indicates too much moisture. The thickness of the biscuit is important; it should not be so thick as to prevent proper drying, or so thin as to crumble in transportation. The quality of stock used for hard bread can be partially told by rules mentioned in the article 'Flour,' as far as they apply. The term 'sprung' is frequently used by bakers, by which is meant raised or flaky bread, indicating strong flour and sound stock. The cupidity of the contracting baker induces him to pack his bread as soon as it comes out of the oven, and before the moisture has been completely expelled by drying. Bread of this kind hangs on breaking; it will also be soft to the pressure of the finger nail when broken, whereas it should be crisp and brittle.

The packages should be thoroughly seasoned, (of wood imparting no taste or odor to the bread,) and reasonably tight. The usual method now adopted is to pack 50 pounds net, in basswood boxes, (sides, top and bottom 1/2 inch, ends 5/8 of an inch,) and of dimensions corresponding with the cutters used, and strapped at each end with light iron or wood. The bread should be packed on its edge compactly, so as not to shake.

Bread thoroughly baked, kiln dried, and packed in spirit casks, will keep a long time but it is an expensive method. If bread contains weevils, or is mouldy, expose to the sun on paulins, and before re-packing it, rinse the barrel with whiskey.

Assistant Commissary General of Subsistence - Lt. Col. C.L. Kilburn: "Notes on Preparing Stores for the United States Army and on the Care of the Same, etc, with a few rules for Detecting Adulterations" - Printed in 1863, by the Government Printing Office, Washington.

Earthworks Beans [24]
Common Fare

1 lb. dried Great Northern Beans – soaked over night, drained, refreshed and boiled until tender, then drained again*
1/4 c. brown sugar
1/4 c. molasses
1 tsp. salt
1 tsp. prepared mustard
2 onions, cut in rings

Combine everything in a greased oven-proof bowl and bake uncovered for 30-40 minutes at 400º.
*You can also use 2 cans of Great Northern Beans, rinsed and drained to make this a quicker recipe to use.

• • • • • • • • •

Trench Beans [27]
Common Fare

1 lb. dry pinto beans
1 Tbl seasoned salt
1 Tbl Worcestershire Sauce
1 Tbl. A-1 Steak Sauce
1/8 tsp. Tabasco
1 tsp. lemon pepper
1 tsp. onion powder
3-4 slices bacon

Soak and cook beans according to package directions. When tender, add other seasonings and simmer until well flavored. Put into greased baking dish and and cover with bacon strips. Bake at 350° for 30-45 minutes until bubbly and bacon cooked.

Rabbit Salad [28]
Officer's Fare

1 rabbit, boiled
Iceberg Lettuce

DRESSING:
yolks of six hard boiled eggs
1 tsp salt
1 tsp pepper
1/4 c. vinegar
1/4 c. prepared mustard
4 Tbl oil

Bread and butter, crackers, grated cheese

Take a fine young rabbit boiled until tender and take the meat from the bones, mincing finely. Also mince an equal portion of lettuce; mix then together and set them aside. Mash the egg yolks very fine, add salt, pepper, vinegar, mustard and oil. Stir together until smooth and pour over rabbit and lettuce. Toss it lightly with a fork, place in serving bowl and serve with bread & butter, crackers, grated cheese.

• • • • • • • • •

Broiled Squirrels [30]
Common Fare

2 squirrels, young and fat
salt & pepper
grated lemon peel
bread crumbs
4 Tbl butter, melted

Case and clean the squirrels, split them open on the back, rinse them very clean in cold water, season them with salt, pepper, and lemon, broil them on a gridiron over coals, turning and basting them 2-3 times with butter. When they are well done, place them in a warm dish and sprinkle with bread crumbs and the rest of the melted butter.

To prepare a hare or rabbit-remove the entrails as soon as dead, and the skin just before cooking. The inside of the body must be kept dry, and it is well to dust it with salt and pepper. To skin them do as follows; cut off legs at first joint, raise the skin on back, draw it over the hind legs and strip it from the tail, then slip it over the fore legs, and cut it away from the head and neck, leaving the ears on the head as perfect as possible. Wash them well, dry with a towel inside and out and proceed to truss them. Cut the sinew of hind legs, turn them towards the head and fasten them to the sides of the rabbit; then turn the fore legs to meet the hind legs, and fasten both with skewers. Push the head back and fasten with skewers. Fill the body with dressing and tie together with string.[29]

Raspberry Cream[31]
Common Fare

2/3 cup Raspberry jam
1 quart heavy cream
Juice of 1 lemon
Sugar
Mix jam into cream and put through a lawn (finely woven thin linen or cotton fabric) sieve. Mix with lemon juice and a little sugar to taste. Whisk until thick. Serve in a dish or glasses.

• • • • • • • • •

Common Custard [32]
Officers' & Common Fare

5 eggs
1 quart milk
Brown sugar
Cinnamon
Nutmeg
Dash of salt

Let milk and eggs come to room temperature. Lightly beat the eggs, then add the milk, and mix. Sweeten to taste with brown sugar. Spice it with a small amount if cinnamon and/or nutmeg and salt. Pour into greased custard cups. Place in a pan of water and bake at 350° for 15-20 minutes or until inserted knife comes out clean.

Puddings and custards were one of the most common desserts in the 1700's and 1800's. Due to the fact that there was limited cooking facilities, a pudding could be cooked and kept warm in a cast iron pot near the fire for hours until needed. Just about everything was used to make a pudding-fruits, vegetables, grains, nuts, and dairy products. Puddings were easy to prepare and inexpensive to make. Richer custards and puddings with expensive ingredients were usually served for "company meals."

Coffee Substitutes[33]
Common Fare

When coffee ran short during the Civil War days, lots of folks from both sides fixed up this sort of drink. They would throw together a handful of whatever kind of grounds were available into the coffee pot, with water, and boil. Egg shells were often tossed into this to settle the grounds.

GROUNDS MATERIALS:
Dry brown bread crumbs
Rye grain soaked in rum
Peas
1 handful small acorns, mixed with 1 handful cracked wheat

All of these substitutes were roasted by themselves and then ground into a coffee. They could also be mixed half and half with real coffee to extend it. Some believed it made the "coffee" richer and clearer if a bit of butter or a whole egg (shell and all) was broken into the coffee substitute and stirred just before it was finished roasting and ground. Sweetener, like honey, was frequently added to make the brew more palatable.

• • • • • • • • •

Raspberry Shrub [34]
Officers' Fare

Raspberries
1 pint of sugar to each pint of raspberry juice
Strong vinegar to barely cover

Put raspberries in a pan and cover them with vinegar. Let stand overnight. Squeeze raspberries through a cheesecloth for clear juice. Add sugar in proportion and test for flavor. Scald resulting juice, skim it and then bottle it when cold.

Shrub is a beverage, but it can also be used for what ever other uses, in cooking, that one wishes to experiment with. Raspberry Shrub can be mixed with water to produce a simple refreshment, or used as an interesting sauce-base, or dressing on salads.

• OTHER FORT FAVORITES •

Canadian Cheese Soup [1]
French-Canadian

1/2 cup carrot, finely chopped
1/4 cup celery, finely chopped
1/4 cup onion, finely chopped
2 Tbl butter
1/4 cup flour

2 cups milk
1 1/2 cups chicken broth
dash paprika
1 1/2 cup cheddar cheese, shredded

Cook carrot, celery, and onion in butter until vegetables are tender. Stir in flour and slowly add chicken broth, milk and paprika. Cook and stir until thick and bubbly. Stir in cheese until melted and serve.

• • • • • • • • •

Chocolate Cake

2 squares of unsweetened baking chocolate
1/2 cup butter
1 1/3 cup of sour milk
2 cups flour

1 heaping cup sugar
1 1/3 tsp baking soda
1/2 tsp salt
1 tsp vanilla

Melt together the chocolate and butter. Mix together the flour, sugar soda and salt. Stir the chocolate mixture and the milk into the dry ingredients. Add the vanilla. Put into a greased 9 x 13 X 2 baking pan. Bake at 350º for 25-35 minutes.

Frosting:
Melt 1/2 square of unsweetened baking chocolate and 1 Tbl of butter and add 1 tsp vanilla. Stir in enough powdered sugar to get to proper frosting consistency. When cake is cooled, frost cake.

Cook's Note: Make sour milk by adding 1 Tbl of vinegar or lemon juice to 1 cup of milk and let stand for 10-15 minutes.

Snickerdoodles [2]

3 1/2 cups flour
1/2 tsp salt
1 1/2 tsp soda
1 1/2 tsp cinnamon
1 1/4 cup butter

1 3/4 cup sugar
3 eggs, slightly beaten
1 cup walnuts, chopped
1 cup raisins

Cream sugar and butter until smooth. Add eggs and beat until smooth. In a separate bowl, combine dry ingredients and add to butter mixture a little at a time. Mix thoroughly. Add nuts and raisins. Drop by teaspoonful onto a greased baking sheet. Bake at 350º for 10-15 minutes.

· · · · · · · · ·

Soft Molasses Cookies [3]

1 cup sugar
1 cup molasses
1 cup butter and lard mixed
1 Tbl soda dissolved in 2/3 cup warm water

1 tsp ginger
pinch salt
4 cups flour

Cream butter/lard and sugar together, add molasses and beat until smooth. In a separate bowl, combine dry ingredients and add a little at a time alternating with the baking soda mixture. Mix thoroughly. These may be baked as either drop cookies or cutouts. Bake on a greased cookie sheet at 450º for 7 minutes.

· · · · · · · · ·

Gingersnap Cookies [4]

2 cups butter and lard mixed
3 cups sugar
3 eggs
3/4 cup molasses

4-5 cups flour
2 1/2 tsp soda
2 1/2 tsp ginger
2 1/2 tsp cinnamon

Beat lard and butter together until creamy. Add 2 1/2 cups sugar and beat until mixture is light and fluffy. Add molasses and eggs and mix well. In a separate bowl mix 4 cups flour and the rest of the dry ingredients. Add dry ingredients a little at a time to the creamed mixture and mix well. If the batter is not stiff enough, add more flour. Make dough into small balls. Roll each in remaining 1/2 cup of sugar and place on greased cookie sheet. Leave enough room for each cookie to spread while baking. Bake at 350º for 15-17 minutes.

Sauerbrauten [5]
German

2 1/2 cups water	1 Tbl sugar
1 1/2 cups red wine vinegar	1 Tbl salt
2 medium onions, sliced	1/4 tsp ground ginger
1/2 lemon, sliced	1 4-pound beef rump roast
12 whole cloves	2 Tbl lard
6 bay leaves	Gingersnap Gravy (see below)*
6 whole black peppercorns	

In a large bowl or crock mix water, vinegar, onions, lemon, cloves, bay leaves, peppercorns, sugar, salt and ginger. Add roast, turning to coat. Cover and refrigerate about 36 hours' Turn meat at least twice daily. Remove meat from marinade; wipe dry. Strain and reserve marinade. In a Dutch oven, brown meat in hot lard; add strained marinade. Cover and simmer till meat is tender, about 2 hours. Remove meat; reserve 1 1/2 cups pan juices.

*Gingersnap Gravy: In a small sauce pan, combine the juices and 1/2 cup hot water; add 2/3 cup broken gingersnaps. Cook, stirring constantly till thick and bubbly. Serve with sauerbrauten.

• • • • • • • • •

Spaetzel or **German Dumplings**

2 cups flour	3/4 cup milk
1 tsp salt	butter
2 eggs (slightly beaten)	dried bread crumbs

Mix flour and salt in a bowl. Add eggs and milk and stir until blended. Drop by spoonfuls into a pot of boiling salted water. Cook for about 5 minutes and drain. Put into a bowl. Stir in butter and mix to coat well. Sprinkle with bread crumbs.

Dumpling Soup
German

2 cups flour
1 egg, well-beaten
1/2 tsp salt

1 3/4 cups cut corn
1 large onion, chopped
5 cups chicken or beef broth

Combine the flour, salt and eggs to make your "dumplings" which will be a very crumbly dough. Cook together the onion, corn and broth until onion is soft. Drop the "dumplings" into the broth and simmer for about 10 minutes.

• • • • • • • • •

Potato Pancakes [6]
German

1/4 cup milk
2 eggs (slightly beaten)
2 Tbl fresh parsley, chopped
3 Tbl flour
1/2 tsp pepper
1 tsp salt

1/2 tsp baking powder
dash ground nutmeg
dash of Worcestershire Sauce
3-4 medium potatoes, peeled (or not)
2 Tbl oil

Mix all ingredients except potatoes and oil together in a bowl. Grate the potatoes directly into the mixture and mix well. Heat spider (skillet) with oil. Drop tablespoons of the batter into the hot oil. Fry until golden brown, then flip to cook other side. Serve hot with applesauce and/or sour cream.

• • • • • • • • •

Corn Fritters
German

1 1/2 cups flour
1/4 tsp pepper
1 tsp salt
2 tsp baking powder

1 Tbl melted butter
2 eggs
1/2 cup milk
2 cups cooked cut corn

Combine flour, salt, pepper and baking powder in bowl. Combine butter, eggs and milk into another bowl and add to dry ingredients. Stir just to mix, add corn and stir again. Drop by spoonfuls onto hot, greased griddle or frying pan. Cook until golden and flip. Serve hot with maple syrup.

Tomato Fritters [7]
German

1 1/2 cups flour
1 tsp sugar
1 tsp baking powder
3/4 tsp salt
1/4 tsp basil
1 Tbl finely minced onion

1/2 tsp Worcestershire Sauce
1 Tbl minced fresh parsley
3 1/2 cups drained whole peeled tomatoes
1 egg, beaten
oil for frying

In a large bowl, combine flour, sugar, baking powder, salt and basil. Cut the tomatoes into 1/2 inch pieces and drain further. Add tomatoes, onion, parsley, Worcestershire Sauce to the flour mixture but do not mix in. Add egg to mixture and blend lightly with a fork. Drop by spoonfuls into a skillet with 1/4 inch hot oil and fry until golden brown. Flip them over and brown the other side. Serve as a breakfast dish with maple syrup or as a vegetable side dish.

• • • • • • • • •

Eggless Cake [8]

1 cup sugar
2 cups flour
1 tsp soda
1 tsp nutmeg
1 tsp cinnamon

1 tsp ground cloves
1 cup sour milk
1/2 cup lard and butter, melted
1 cup raisins, well-floured

Combine dry ingredients. Add sour milk and lard/butter mixture. Mix. Add raisins. Pour batter into well greased pan. Bake at 350º for 30 minutes until done.

Cook's Note: To make sour milk if none is on hand, use 1 Tbl. vinegar or lemon juice in 1 cup milk and let stand for 10-15 minutes.

• • • • • • • • •

Blueberry Cake

1 cup sugar
1/3 cup oil
1 egg
1 heaping tsp baking soda

1/2 tsp salt
1 cup sour milk
2 cups flour
1-1 1/2 cups blueberries

Mix sugar, oil and egg together. Add soda, salt and sour milk and mix well. Stir in flour a little at a time and when well mixed, gently fold in blueberries. Pour into well greased 8 X 8 inch pan and bake at 350º for 30 minutes.

Cook's Note: Other fruits have been used in this cake as well as adding nuts to the batter. One especially good choice is to cut fresh cranberries in half and coat them with about 1/4 cup sugar and grate in 2 tsp of orange peel.

Nothing Cake [9]

1 1/2 cups brown sugar
1/2 tsp salt
1 cup sour milk
1/2 cup butter
1 egg

2 1/2 cups flour
1 tsp baking soda
cinnamon, nutmeg, cloves, allspice-whatever
    spice you prefer or combination there of may be
    added to enhance the flavor

Mix butter, flour and sugar together until crumbly. Take half the crumbs and set them aside. Add baking soda and salt to the milk. Mix with one half of crumbs. Beat in the egg. Pour batter into well greased pan and sprinkle remaining crumbs on top. Bake at 350º for 30 minutes.

Cook's Note: We do not know for certain how this cake got its name. Probably because it had no fruits or spices added to it. It is "nothing" special. This cake is a favorite of the soldiers of the Old Fort Niagara Guard. They think it is called "nothing cake" because, soon after it comes out of the Dutch oven, there is nothing left!

· · · · · · · · ·

Cinnamon Flop [10]

Topping:
1 cup brown sugar
4 Tbl softened butter
1/2 tsp cinnamon

Batter:
2 cups flour
2 tsp baking powder
1/2 tsp salt
1/2 cup sugar

2 Tbl softened butter
1 egg, well-beaten
1 cup milk
peaches or apples

Topping: Work brown sugar, butter, and cinnamon until crumbly.

Batter: Mix flour, baking powder, and salt together. Cream sugar and butter in a separate bowl and add egg until well mixed. Stir in milk and flour. Pour into a greased 9 inch round pan and sprinkle the topping over the surface. Peaches or apples may also be diced and scattered on top. Fruit may be added to the batter as well. Bake in 425 º oven for 30-35 minutes. Butter will melt while baking so it is best to put a pan underneath to catch the drippings. Served warm, this makes a delicious breakfast bread.

Sally Lunn [11]

2 cups flour	2 eggs, separated
3 tsp baking powder	1/2 cup milk
1/2 tsp salt	1/2 cup melted butter

Mix and sift the dry ingredients. Add milk to the beaten egg yolks and add this mixture to the dry ingredients, stirring until just mixed. Stir in melted butter, then fold in the stiffly beaten egg whites. Bake in a well-greased 9 inch pan in a moderate oven (350º) for about 30 minutes.

• • • or • • •

1 pkg dry yeast	3 Tbl sugar
1/4 cup warm water	2 eggs
3/4 cup warm milk	3 cups flour
6 Tbl butter	1 1/4 tsp salt

In a small bowl, soften yeast in warm water Add warm milk and set aside. In a large bowl, cream butter and sugar and add eggs one at a time, beating well in between. Sift together the flour and salt and add to creamed mixture alternating with yeast mixture. Beat well after each addition. Beat batter till smooth. Cover batter and let rise in a warm place until double (1 hour). Beat down and pour batter into a well-greased Turk's head mold or 9 inch tube pan. Let rise in a warm place till almost double (about 30 minutes). Bake at 350º for 40-45 minutes. Remove bread from mold or tube pan. Serve either warm or cool.

Cooks' Note: The origin of "Sally Lunn" has many stories. One is that it evolved from the French words for sun & moon ("soleil-lune") – the top would turn golden brown while the bottom would remain white resembling the sun and the moon. The other is about an English girl, Sally Lunn who sold the baked goods in Bath. It was baked in the Turk's head mold by the time it came to America and was very popular for tea. [12]

• • • • • • • • •

Boston Brown Bread [13]

2 cups sour milk	2 cups whole wheat flour
1/2 cup molasses	1 1/2 tsp soda
2 cups flour	scant tsp salt

Combine ingredients. Divide dough and place in two 1 quart buttered pudding molds. Fill each mold 3/4 full. Cover molds with butter lids. Lids must be secured tightly to prevent lifting. Place pudding molds in a pan with water halfway up the mold. Steam 3 hours in the oven at 350º and bake 1/2 hour out of the water. Coffee cans covered with aluminum foil may be used if pudding molds are unavailable.

Hobnails [14]

1 cup brown sugar
1/2 cup lard (or margarine)
1 well-beaten egg
1 tsp vanilla
1 1/2 cups flour

1/2 tsp salt
1/2 cup raisins
1/2 tsp baking soda
1 tsp cinnamon

Cream together sugar, lard, egg and vanilla. Stir together dry ingredients. Add to creamed mixture a little at a time. Form into small balls. Place on greased baking sheet about 3 inches apart. Bake at 350º for 12-15 minutes.

· · · · · · · · ·

Raisin Bread [15]

1 pkg yeast
2 1/2 cups warm water
2 tsp salt
2 tsp cinnamon

1/2 cup honey
2 cups raisins
6-7 cups flour

Mix 3 cups flour with salt and cinnamon. Dissolve yeast in 1 cup warm water. Pour into flour mixture. Mix thoroughly and add honey and raisins. Alternately add remaining flour and water. Knead dough at least 10 minutes. Set in a warm place to rise until dough is doubled (about 1 hour). Punch down and let rise a second time. Punch down once more and bake at 350º for approximately 1 hour. This dough can be divided into 3 loaves and baked about 35-45 minutes each. This way they fit in the Dutch oven.

· · · · · · · · ·

Suet Pudding [16]

1 cup chopped suet
1 cup milk
1 cup molasses
1 cup chopped raisins

3 cups flour
1 tsp soda
dash of salt

Combine ingredients. Place in a cheese cloth and steam over a pot of boiling water for 2 hours.

Pumpkin Pie [17]

1 unbaked pie shell
2 cups cooked pumpkin
2/3 cup brown sugar (packed firmly)
2 tsp cinnamon
1 tsp allspice

1/2 tsp ginger
1/2 tsp nutmeg
1/4 cup butter, softened
3/4 cup milk
2 well-beaten eggs

Combine pumpkin, sugar and spices in a large bowl. Beat in milk, eggs and butter until fluffy. Pour into pie shell and bake at 450º for 10 minutes-turn down oven to 325º and continue baking for approximately 45-50 minutes more. Knife will come out clean when inserted to test for doneness.

• • • • • • • • •

Ghost Cookies [18]
(Popular Tuscarora Indian Recipe)

2 cups sugar
1 1/2 cup shortening
3 eggs
2 tsp vanilla
1 cup milk

4-6 cups flour
5 tsp baking powder
2 tsp nutmeg
1 cup raisins or walnuts

Cream sugar and shortening; add eggs and beat until fluffy. Sift together 3 cups flour, baking powder, nutmeg. Add vanilla to milk. Stir flour mixture and milk mixture into creamed ingredients by alternating back and forth until well blended. Add enough flour so that dough can be rolled out to 1/3 inch thick and cut into circles. Bake at 375º for 8-10 minutes.

• • • • • • • • •

Eggless Coffee Cake (legacy)

2 cups strong brewed coffee
1 1/2 cups white sugar
1/2 cup butter
1 cup raisins
1 tsp ground allspice

1 tsp ground cinnamon
3 cups all-purpose flour
2 tsp baking soda
1 tsp baking powder

Preheat oven to 350º F. Grease and flour a 9x13 inch pan. Sift together the flour, baking soda and baking powder; set aside. Combine the coffee, sugar, butter, raisins, allspice and cinnamon in a large pot, then bring to a boil; remove from heat and set aside to cool to room temperature. Stir the flour mixture into the cooled liquid until well combined. Pour into pan and bake in preheated oven for 45 to 50 minutes, or until a toothpick comes out clean.

Sobronade (legacy)
(A French Soup)

4 cups of cooked navy beans
2 cups of Ham, diced
2 medium onions, diced
2 large potatoes, diced
4 medium carrots, diced
4 ribs celery, diced

1 tsp garlic, minced
3 quarts water
2 bay leafs
2 tsp thyme
2 Tbl parsley

Combine all ingredients in a large pot, and bring to a boil, slowly. Reduce heat and simmer for approximately 1 hour on a medium fire. Great with a good piece of bread. Serves 6-8.

• • • • • • • • •

French-Canadian Baked Beans (legacy)

1 lb small white pea beans, dry
1 onion, coarsely chopped
1 tsp dry mustard
salt to taste

1 to 2 tsp ground black pepper
1 to 2 cups pure maple syrup, plus more if desired
1/3 to 1/2 pound of salt pork
water

Pick-over beans and remove bad ones and stones. Place beans in a bowl and cover well, with water, and soak overnight. Drain beans and place in 4-quart bean pot. Add onion, dry mustard, pepper, salt, and maple syrup. Add water to cover. Cut salt pork into 1-inch pieces and place on top of beans. Bake, covered, for approximately 8 hours in a 250° oven or fire pit. Check the pot each hour to see if water needs to be added, otherwise the beans will dry out too much and will be impossible to eat. Additional maple syrup can be added, in place of water, to intensify the flavor. Serve with ham or other items of your choosing. Also good with eggs and bacon for breakfast, or with toast.

• • • • • • • • •

Venison and Barley Soup (legacy)

2 gallons of water
2 to 3 lb venison, cut up in cubes
2 rutabagas, diced
4 carrots, sliced
4 ribs celery, diced

1 large onion - diced
salt & pepper to taste
2 to 3 cups of barley
2 tomatoes (optional), diced

Place the venison in a large pot, add water, and bring to a boil. Add the vegetables and seasoning, continue cooking for about 45 minutes, then add the barley and cook for another 30 minutes until all oof the ingredients are tender. Adjust seasoning and water as needed.

Venison Sausage [legacy]

3 lb venison
1 lb pork
3 tsp sage, dried and crushed

3 tsp salt
3 tsp black pepper

Chop and mince, or grind the meats; combine. Add the sage, salt, and black pepper; mix all thoroughly. Make it into small flat cakes, and fry until cooked through, or put into casings and cook as desired. To make a larger quantity at the same time, simply multiply the quantities accordingly.

• • • • • • • • •

Venison and Ale Stew [legacy]

2 lb venison
3 Tbl flour
Salt and pepper to taste
2 Tbl oil
2 cups onions, diced
1 1/2 cups carrots, diced

1 teaspoon garlic (fresh), minced
1/2 cup tomatoes, crushed well
1 cup stout ale (a dark ale works well)
2 cups broth (beef works best)
1/2 tsp thyme

Heat oil in a heavy skillet. Combine the flour, salt and pepper in a large bowl, add the venison, and toss to coat well. Then brown the meat well in the oil. Add the remaining ingredients to the skillet, and slowly bring to a boil; reduce heat and simmer until the venison is really tender (approx. 1 hour, or longer), adding more broth if necessary to maintain liquidity of your liking. If venison is unavailable, beef may be substituted.

• • • • • • • • •

Potato Sausage [legacy]
(Variation on a Swedish version)

5 lb potatoes, ground
6 lb ground pork
4 lb ground beef
1 1/2 onions, diced

6 Tbl salt
1 tsp pepper
1 1/2 tsp allspice
casings (optional)

Combine the meats together, then add potatoes and mix well. Next, add spices and mix all thoroughly, then form into patties, or stuff in casings. If using casings, sausage can be boiled first then fried in some butter in a skillet over a medium heat. Patties can be skillet fried in some butter as well.

Irish Soda Bread [legacy]

4 cups bleached all-purpose flour	1 tsp salt
1 tsp baking soda	2 cups buttermilk

Combine the flour, baking soda, and salt in a large mixing bowl and stir to combine thoroughly. Next, form a "well" in the middle, and add the buttermilk; mix gently. Transfer the dough to a lightly floured board, and gently fold the edges into each other four times, turn over so that fold-side is on the bottom, then pat the dough out into a circle about nine inches in diameter and about one inch thick. With a sharp knife, make two long slashes in the shape of a cross on the top. Place on griddle over hot coals and cook until done. If you prefer to bake in an oven: preheat oven to 450 degrees (f). Place the dough in a lightly grease 10-inch round cake pan, and bake for 15 minutes. Reduce the oven temperature to 400° and continue bake until the bread is brown (approximately 25 minutes) and sounds hollow when thumped. Remove pan from the oven, then place the bread on a wire rack to cool. Actual baking time can vary quite a bit by oven, so keep an eye on it and adjust accordingly; it may not take as long.

• • • • • • • • •

Election Cake [legacy]
(Noted as being from "The American Frugal Housewife" by Mrs. Lydia Child, 1833)

4 lb flour	1 lb currants or raisins
3/4 lb butter	1 package yeast (*modern equivalent for this recipe)
4 eggs	Milk
1 lb sugar	

"Old fashioned election cake is made of four pounds of flour; three quarters of a pound of butter; four eggs, one pound of sugar; one pound of currants, or raisins if you choose; half a pint of good yeast*; wet it with milk as soft as it can be and be moulded on a board. Set to rise over night in winter; in warm weather, three hours is usually enough for it to rise. A loaf, the size of common flour bread, should bake three quarters of an hour."...L. Child, 1833

• • • • • • • • •

Cider Cake [legacy]
(Noted as being from "The American Frugal Housewife" by Mrs. Lydia Child, 1833)

1 1/2 lb flour	1/2 pint cider
1/2 lb sugar	1 tsp baking powder
1/4 lb butter	Spices as desired

"Cider cake is very good, to be baked in small loaves. One pound and a half of flour, half a pound of sugar, quarter of a pound of butter, half a pint of cider, one teaspoon of pearlash; spice to your taste. Bake till it turns easily in the pans. I should think about half an hour." ...L. Child, 1833

Hard Biscuits for Hunting Trips [legacy]
(Hardtack variation – Northern New York and Quebec)

2 cups flour
1/3 cup maple syrup
3/4 tsp salt

3 Tbl shortening
1/4 tsp baking soda
6 Tbl buttermilk

Combine the flour, salt, then cut in the shortening; add the maple syrup and mix. In a separate bowl, mix together the baking soda and buttermilk, then add it immediately to the flour combination. Mix it all well. Roll it out very thin and score the dough in rectangles, without cutting through; prick each rectangle several times with a fork or toothpick. Bake as soon as possible on an ungreased cookie sheet, at 425° for 5-10 minutes or until golden brown.

During the production of this book, a member of the Old Fort Niagara Publications Committee, *Dean Ford Ulrich*, passed away, from cancer. The following recipe is presented in his memory, as it was one of his all-time favorites. In the early 1980s, Dean and I had the chance to pay an extended research-visit to Old Fort William in Thunder Bay, Ontario, Canada. Bread was, and still is, fresh-baked on site (hearth), and the (c.1816) recipe freely shared with visitors. Staff members who worked as bakers were extremely helpful, and their kindness was never forgotten. The wording, that follows, is somewhat different from the original Old Fort William handout, but the information is all there. *Thank You,* Old Fort William. *Thank You,* JoAnn, for including this recipe. *Thank You,* Dean, for your dedicated service to Old Fort Niagara.....*Harry M. DeBan, Publisher.*

Whole Wheat Bread-Fort William (c.1816)

3 cups (total) lukewarm water
5 Tbl (total) white sugar
2 Tbl yeast
1 1/2 tsp salt

1/2 cup lard
3 cups whole wheat flour
4 cups white flour

Dissolve 1 Tbl of white sugar into 1 cup of the warm water, then add the yeast and let brew for 10 minutes. In a large bowl, mix all of the flour, the remaining 4 Tbl of sugar, and the salt, then rub in the the lard until smooth. Next, pour in the yeast mixture, then add the remaining 2 cups of water and mix well. Turn the dough onto a floured board and knead for 10 minutes (the dough should be fairly stiff, but manageable). Place dough into a greased bowl, cover, and let rise until double in size. Punch the dough down, then divide and form into 2 or 3 loaves. Place into greased pans and let rise until doubled again. Bake in a pre-heated 375° oven for 30 to 40 minutes, depending on the size of the loaves, but watch carefully the first time and adjust temperature and/or time if necessary for your particular oven (no lower than 350° F). *Time could be substantially less.* Be patient working out the times and temperatures for this recipe...the bread is worth it, especially warm out of the oven!

Cook's Note: If you have access to a baking stone or other hearth type of oven, and do not want to use baking pans: form the dough into rounds (after punching it down) and let rise (final rise), covered, on a floured board until doubled again in size. Place on stone in a pre-heated 350° F oven for 30-40 minutes, depending on the size of the loaves, or until done (watch carefully the first time and adjust as needed). *Time could be substantially less.* You can use some corn meal as a release-aid on the stone and bread peel.

• Glossary •

Ale: An English term for dark, heavy, bitter beer.

Andiron: A metal support for firewood, used in a fireplace hearth.

Baking Powder: A powder used as leavening in quick breads and cakes. The two main ingredients are baking soda and an acid such as cream of tartar. When moistened, they produce carbon dioxide, causing the dough the dough to rise.

Baking Soda: A white powder, sodium bicarbonate, that reacts with an acid to produce carbon dioxide. This raises the dough during baking.

Barm: A homemade yeast that is made from the froth that forms on top of fermenting ale which is stored in a stone jar in a cool place.

Bateau (pl. bateaux): A flat-bottomed, double ended boat used on the lakes and rivers of northern North America by the French, British and Americans for the movement of men and supplies.

Barrel: A large, staved, wooden cask used for the shipment of goods. The standard weight of the barrels of flour and pork sent by the British to Fort Niagara was 215 pounds.

Brine: A solution of salt and water, used for pickling. This was used for preserving meats as well as making different types of pickled vegetables in the eighteenth century.

Cream of Tartar: A white, crystal, potassium bitartrate, crushed to a powder, acid in taste and action. It is made from the scrapings of wine vats. When it is combined with baking soda it makes baking powder.

Dram (or drahm): A unit of measurement equal to one eighth of an ounce.

Dutch Oven: An iron pot with legs and a lid with a lip on it. This is so coals can be put on the lid without sliding off and underneath for baking.

Firkin: A small wooden cask which holds butter or cheese, larger at the bottom than on top. It was one quarter of a barrel in measurement or 66 3/4 pounds in "Canadian weight" during the British period.

Freshen: The process of removing salt from preserved fish or meat by soaking in several baths of fresh water.

Gill: A measure of one quarter of a pint which is 4 fluid ounces (1/2 cup).

Gridiron: A metal grill or grid, used over coals for grilling fish or meat.

Grog: A combination of hot water and rum which was served to the British navy in the mid 1700s to prevent scurvy.

Hardtack: A hard biscuit, made with flour and water only, also called a *sea biscuit, tooth-dullers, sheet iron,* and c*rown breakers.*

Hominy: Hulled corn, corn which was soaked in lye water to remove the skin leaving the soft inner kernel of corn.

Isinglass: A high quality gelatin which was made by melting the swimming bladders of sturgeon.

Jerusalem Artichoke: An American sunflower widely cultivated for its tubers. It was used as a vegetable and livestock feed, and commonly known as "Indian Potatoes".

Kettle: A commonly used cooking pot of the eighteenth century. Today we would use a saucepan in its place.

Lye: A strong alkaline solution obtained by running water through wood ash. It was used in soap making as well as used to soak the husks off corn for hominy.

Mortar and Pestle: A bowl and pounding tool used to grind coffee, spices, herbs, salt and sugar.

Pearl Ash: An early form of baking powder, obtained from wood and plant ashes used as an early form of leavening (also called "potash").

Pease (pl. peasen): An early name for peas.

Peck: A measure for dry goods which equals 1/4 of a bushel or two gallons.

Peel: A large handled wooden paddle used ot move food, especially bread, in and out of a brick oven.

Pickle: A brine or vinegar solution, used to preserve meat or produce.

Pipkin: A wooden bucket with one stave longer than the other to serve as a handle. It was used fro dipping from a tub or vat

.

Porringer: A dish made of cast iron, pewter or silver which was used to warm and serve small quantities of food.

Ration: The amount of food designated by the army to be issued to one man for one day.

Reflector Oven: (tin kitchen) a sheet metal reflector box, open on one side facing the fire, used to reflect the heat back. It was used for roasting or baked goods.

Rosewater: A flavoring extract made from rose petals and liquor.

S-Hook: An "S" shaped hook used to hang pots over the fire. Usually one would have three or four of them to be able to raise or lower the pot as needed to increase or reduce the amount of heat needed for cooking.

Sagamite: A common meal of the voyageurs which consisted of mush with game or fish added when available.

Salamander: a long handled, flat disk or iron, which was heated in the fire and then quickly passed over the a dish of food to brown the top.

Sallet: Salad.

Salt Peter: Potassium nitrate which is added to meats to preserve its color.

Salteratus: An early form of baking soda.

Shallot: An onion like vegetable which is in the garlic family but milder. It is used for seasoning and in pickles.

Shrub: Rum or brandy with sugar and spices added which is poured over fruit.

Spider: A cooking pan which resembles a modern skillet with three long legs which allows it to stand over a fire.

Spit: An iron spear pointed rod for holding and turning meat while roasting over a fire.

Sponge: A dough that has been raised and turn into a light, porous mass by the action of yeast.

Spruce Beer: A beer brewed by using molasses and spruce tips. This was a common beverage for the soldiers and common folk because it was used to prevent scurvy.

Tierce: A wooden cask used for the shipment of rice and peas during the British period. The normal weight was 531 pounds.

Trammel: An iron gadget with slots, hinge on a crane and used to suspend pots over a fire.

Trencher: An early wooden plate which had an indentation carved into it or a small oblong bowl, which kept gravies or sauces from spilling.

Trivet: A flat cast iron piece of metal made in various shapes with three legs attached. It was used as a base for flat bottomed pots to allow them to be put over the fire. Smaller ones could be placed in a Dutch oven to raise a pie or cake tin off the bottom to allow the air to circulate.

Appendix: Faunal Remains
Animals Represented in the
*Old Fort Niagara Fauna Collection**

Extensive archaeological excavations were carried out at Old Fort Niagara from 1979-1991 under the co-directorship of Stuart D. Scott, Ph.D and Patricia Kay Scott. The faunal material collected were identified by Dr. Steven Cumba, Dr. Elizabeth Scott, Dr. Elizabeth Wing, and Irvy Quitmeyer.

Several in-depth studies of the faunal material have been undertaken that showed in general that the French relied more on wild food sources than did the British or American occupants of the Fort. In many cases, these animal bones excavated from 1979 through 1991 could only be identified as representing either mammals, birds, fish, reptiles, or amphibians. Other bones were able to be classified more fully to a particular animal order or family such as: the Old World mouse/rat family; New World mouse and rat family; the even-toed ungulant order; perching bird order; vulture, hawk and falcon order; tern subfamily; cod family; or poisonous snake family. However, even with the fragmented nature of most of the faunal material, the following animals were able to be fully identified.

* The listing by common names is included solely for the purpose of showing the diversity of wild and domestic animal remains found on the historic site. It is not intended to identify specific remains with specific eras of the Fort's history, or to necessarily indicate consumption by humans. Archaeological excavations and research continue at Fortress Niagara to the present day, and with each excavation, new species of animals are discovered in the subsurface cultural deposits.

deer mouse
brown or Norway rat
snowshoe hare
eastern cottontail
ground hog (woodchuck)
gray squirrel
fox squirrel
eastern chipmunk
beaver
muskrat
vole
porcupine
dog, coyote, or wolf
fox
black bear
raccoon
skunk
domestic cat

bobcat
horse
domestic swine (pig)
American elk
white-tail deer
moose
elk or wapiti (red deer)
bison
domestic cow
sheep
big brown bat
perching bird
American robin
finch
common raven
grebe family
pied-billed grebe
horned grebe

Faunal remains (continued)...

Canada goose
wood duck
anas duck
northern pintail
American widgeon
gadwall
green or blue-winged teal
mallard or black duck s
northern shoveler
ring-necked duck
lesser scaup
canvasback
buffehead
merganser
red-brested merganser
hooded merganser
bald eagle
red-tailed hawk
buzzard hawk
American kestrel
great horned owl
snowy owl
domestic chicken
ruffed grouse
wild turkey
sandhill crane
shorebird order
sandpiper and phalarope family
sandpiper
killdeer
Wilson's phalarope
greater yellowlegs
gull
herring gull
passenger pigeon
mourning dove
belted kingfisher
pileated woodpecker
sturgeon or gar
lake sturgeon

freshwater eel
sucker
redhorse
freshwater catfish
yellow bullhead
brown bullhead
flathead catfish
channel catfish
stonecat
northern pike
muskellunge
lake trout
whitefish
round whitefish
lake whitefish
burbot
spotter or long-nosed gar
perch family
yellow perch
smallmouth bass
largemouth bass
white bass
rock bass
sunfish
white crappie
walleye
freshwater drum
Atlantic salmon
bowfin
northern water snake
painted turtle
snapping turtle
frog
toad
clam
snail

• Index of Recipes (by Category) •

. . . *continued next page* . . .

• Notes •

Introduction & French (1726-1759)

1. Hallatt, Mary Catherine & Lipa, Lynn M., *The King's Bread*, pp. 4-5
2. Farmer, Dennis & Farmer, Carol, *The King's Bread, 2d Rising.* p.21
3. Farmer & Farmer, p. 21
4. Gray, Paula. "Great Grains for Breakfast." Online posting. 14 March 01. <http://www.coopfoodstore.com /pages/topics/grains/html>
5. Hallatt & Lipa, p. 12
6. Farmer & Farmer, p. 8
7. Louisbourg Institute. *Behind the Scenes at the Fortress of Louisbourg.* 05/14/01. <http://w3.uccb.ns.ca/behind/broth.html>
8. Tanguy, Yannig. Crown Point Bread Company, personal communication
9. Farmer & Farmer, p. 7
10. Famer & Farmer, pp. 33-34
11. Dunnigan, Brian Leigh, *Memoirs on the Late Wat in North America Between France and England,* p. 139
12. Scott, Elizabeth M., *French Subsistencen at Fort Michilimackinac, 1715-1781; The Clergy and the Traders,* pp. 24-25
13. Thwaites, Reuben Gold, *The Jesuit Relations*, Vol. XV, p. 163
14. Parker, Arthur C., "Iroquois Uses of Maize and other Food Plants.",p. 69
15. Wheaton, Barbara Ketcham, *Savoring the Past: The French Kitchen and Table from 1300 to 1789,* pp. 208-09
16. Benson, Adoph, B. (ed.), Peter Kalm's travels in North America: *The English Version of 1770,* p. 702
17. Hallatt & Lipa, p. 22
18. Benson, p. 702
19. Syfert, Marguerite, L. *From the Hearths of Fort Stanwix,* p. 21
20. Benson, p. 707
21. Scott, Elizabeth, p. 9
22. Scott, Patricia & Stuart
23. Kent, Donald H. , *The French Invasion of Western Pennsylvania, 1753,* pp. 30-31
24. Wheaton, p. 244
25. Cormier-Boudreau & Gallant p. 158
26. Hallatt & Lipa, p. 10
27. Better Homes and Gardens , *Heritage Cook Book,* p. 248

<u>*Notes*</u> *(continued)...*

28. Farmer & Farmer, p. 30
29. Wheaton, pp. 262-263; Haldimand, Frederick, Manuscript papers of General Frederick Haldimand, Add. MSS 21661-21892, MSS 21760, Sept. 9, 1779
30. Mitchell, Patricia B., *French Cooking in Early America*, p. 24
31. Cormier-Boudreau, Marielle, Gallant, Melvin. *La Cuisine Acadienne*, p.37
32. Cormier-Boudreau & Gallant, p. 27
33. Cormier-Boudreau & Gallant, p. 29
34. Cormier-Boudreau & Gallant, p.150
35. Cormier-Boudreau & Callant, p. 157
36. Cormier-Boudreau & Gallant, p. 157
37. Eustice, Sally, *History from the Hearth, p. 54*
38. Cormier-Boudreau & Gallant p. 25
39. Eustice, Sally, *pp. 50-51*
40. Eustice, Sally, *pp. 51-52*
41. Hallat & Lipa, p. 9

British (1760-1775)

1. Farmer & Farmer, pp. 13-15
2. Farmer & Farmer, p. 12
3. Farmer & Farmer, pp. 31-32
4. Farmer & Farmer, p. 32
5. Hallatt & Lipa, p. 19
6. Farmer & Farmer, p. 50
7. Hallat & Lipa, p. 18
8. Gage, Thomas. Manuscript papers of General Thomas Gage, 1759-1775. ; Haldimand, Add, MSS 21760, Sept. 9, 1799.
9. Child, Mrs. *The American Frugal Housewife.* (1833) p. 83
10. Fitch, Jabez Jr. *The Diary of Jabez Fitch Jr in the French and Indian War, 1757.* pp.2-3; Haldimand, Add. MSS 21760, Sept. 9, 1779; Flick, Alexander C. "New Sources on the Sullivan-Clinton Campaign in 1779." p. 68; Forsyth, George. Manuscript account book, 1780, RG10, Vol. 1838.
11. Hallatt & Lipa, p. 20
12. Sloat, Caroline, *Old Sturbridge Village Cookbook.* pp. 90-91; Gage, Vol.5, March 18, 1760
13. Hallatt & Lipa p. 22
14. Gage, Vol. 6, May 8, 1760
15. Sloat, p. 206-07
16. Langton, H. H. (ed.). *Patrick Campbell: Travels in North America.* p. 147
17. Sloat p. 206-207
18. Hallatt & Lipa p. 22

<u>*Notes*</u> *(continued)...*

19. Sulivan, James and Hamilton, Milton W. (eds.). *The Papers of Sir William Johnson.* p. 694
20. Hallat & Lipa, p. 42
21. Farmer & Farmer, p. 9
22. Sullivan and Hamilton, pp.566-67 and 603-05: Patricia and Stuart Scott Hallat & Lipa p. 21
23. Child, p. 55
24. Child, p. 55
25. Patricia and Stuart Scott
26. Hallatt & Lipa, p.42
27. Fisher, Jabez M. Manuscript Journal of Jabez M. Fisher, June, July & August 1773. p. 47; Gage, Vol.5, Feb.2, 1790; Inis, Mary Quayle (ed.). *Mrs. Simcoe's Diary.* p. 165
28. Sloat, pp.82-83
29. Gage, Vol.4, Nov. 19, 1759; Patricia and Stuart Scott
30. Simmons, p. 152
31. Eustice, p. 153
32. Hallatt & Lipa, p. 21
33. Gage, Vol. 71, Oct. 25, 1767
34. Better Homes and Gardens, p. 30
35. Better Homes and Gardens, p. 30
36. Wood, Emma. *Antique Dinner Recipes for All Seasons.* p. 33
37. Simmons, pp. 11-12
38. Hallatt & Lipa, p. 28
39. Isabella Graham Correspondence, George Duffield Papers
40. Bowler, R.A., ed., Rundell, Mrs. Maria Eliza. *A New System of Domestic Cookery by Mrs. Maria Eliza Rundell.* p. 233
41. Isabella Graham
42. Hallatt & Lipa p. 33
43. Farmer & Farmer, p. 15
44. Better Homes and Gardens, p,135
45. Benson, pp 173-174
46. Better Homes and Gardens , p.84
47. Simmons, p. 32
48. Better Homes and Gardens, American Heritage Cookbook , p. 92
49. Fisher, p. 42
50. Hallatt & Lipa, p. 47
51. Sloat, pp. 144-45
52. Grose, Frances. *A Dictionary of Buckish Slang, University Wit, and Pickpocket Eloquence,* p.HAZ
53. Hallatt & Lipa, p. 48

<u>Notes</u> *(continued)...*

Revolutionary War(1775-1796)

1. Farmer & Farmer, pp. 54-57
2. Hallatt & Lipa, p. 19
3. Farmer & Farmer, p. 57
4. Burgoyne, p. 43
5. Kavach, Barrie. *Native Harvests, Recipes and Botanicals of the American Indian.* pp. 129-138
6. Haldimand, Add. MSS, 21760, Sept. P, 1779; Innis, p.184.
7. Simmons, p. 62
8. Innis, p. 163
9. Hallatt & Lipa, p. 33
10. Child, p. 69; Hallatt & Lipa, p. 33
11. Sloat, pp. 210-11
12. Wright and Tinling, p. 80
13. Simmons, p. 55-57; Child, p. 69
14. Inis, p. 97
15. Burgoyne, pp. 11-12
16. Eustice, p. 132
17. Eustice, p. 133
18. Lowell, p. 151
19. Eustice, p. 132
20. Hallatt & Lipa, p. 20
21. Sloat, p. 45
22. Innis, p. 81
23. Better Homes and Gardens, p. 52
24. Child, p. 70
25. Simmons, p. 36
26. Rundle p. 194
27. Grose, p. FLY; Sime, pp. 82-83
28. Hallatt & Lipa, p. 47
29. Hallatt & Lipa, p. 48
30. Hallatt & Lipa, p. 39; Eustice, p.115
31. Rundle, pp. 233-234; Glasse, p. 317
32. Better Homes and Gardens , p. 227; Eustice, p. 106
33. Burgoyne, Bruce, *A Hessian Diary of the American Revolution by Johann Conrad Döhla.* p.144
34. Better Homes and Gardens , p.28
35. Burgoyne, p. 185
36. Bowler, p. 69
37. Burgoyne, Bruce. *George Pausch's Journal and Reports of the Campaign in America.* p.43
38. Fitch, p. 2

<u>*Notes*</u> *(continued)...*

39. Sloat, p. 115
40. Weld, Isaac Jr. *Travels through the States of North America and the Provinces of Upper and Lower Canada during the years 1795-1797.* pp. 149-50
41. Burgoyne, *A Hessian Diary,* p. 35
42. Fisher, p. 49
43. Personal communication with Francene Patterson, Tuscaroran Native American
44. Parker, p. 68
45. Eustice, p. 124
46. Parker p. 78
47. Encyclopediapopcornica. "RE: Popcorn." Online posting. 27 March 2001. <hww.popcorn.org/encyclopedia/eppophs.cfm>.
48. Parker, p. 90
49. Parker, p. 92
50. Parker, p. 68
51. Parker, p. 92
52. Moses, Verna S. *Heap Good' Cookin' Tonawanda Indian Baptist Church Cookbook p. 31*
53. Moses, Verna S., p. 33
54. Farnham, Rose, personal communication
55. Moses, Verna S., p.31

American (1796-1872)

1. Farmer & Farmer, p.74
2. Dunnigan, Brian. *A History and guide to Old Fort Niagara.* pp.18022
3. Farmer & Farmer, p. 74
4. Dunnigan, pp. 23-26
5. Bell, Irvin Wiley, *The Life of Billy Yank: The Common Soldier. p.224*
6. Simmons, p. 38
7. Scott, Winfield. *General Regulations for the Army.* p. 7
8. Scott, Winfield, p.44
9. Carlo, Joyce W, *Trammels, Trenchers, & Tartlets.* pp. 91-92
10. Weld, p. 86
11. Carlo, p. 92
12. McFeely,George. Order book of Lt. Col, George McFeely, 1812-1813. pp. 21-23
13. Sanderson, Capt. James M. *Camp Fires and Camp Cooking:or Culinary Hints for the Soldier* p. 9
14. Rundell, p. 156
15. Rundell, p. 155
16. Rundell, p. 156
17. Rundell, p. 214
18. McFeely, p. 93

<u>*Notes*</u> *(continued)...*

19. Better Homes & Gardens, p. 76
20. Farmer & Farmer, p. 74
21. Mitchell, Patricia B. *Union Army Camp Cooking, 1861-1865.* p. 29
22. Billings, John D. *Hardtack and Coffee: the Unwritten Story of Army Life.* pp.218-219
23. 1860's Foods *Union, Confederate, & on the Frontier.* p. 4
24. Mitchell, p. 26
25. Small, Harold, ed., *the Road to Richmond: The Civil Wat Memoirs of Major Abner R. Small of the 16th Maine Vounteers,* pp. 192-193
26. Billings, pp. 218-219
27. Mitchell, p. 26
28. Civil War Interactive, *The CWi Civil War Cookbook,* Wild Game, pp. 1-2
29. Civil War Interactive, *The CWi Civil War Cookbook,* Wild Game, p. 2
30. Civil War Interactive, *The CWi Civil War Cookbook,* Wild Game, p. 2
31. *1860's Foods* (Bowman, ed.), p. 8
32. *1860's Foods* (Bowman, ed.), p. 8
33. *1860's Foods* (Bowman, ed.), pp. 1-2
34. *1860's Foods* (Bowman, ed.), p. 2

Other Fort Favorites

1. Better Homes & Gardens, p. 245
2. Hallatt & Lipa, p. 37
3. Hallatt & Lipa, p. 32
4. Hallatt & Lipa, p. 37
5. Better Homes & Gardens, p. 69
6. Adams, p. 191
7. Adams, p. 35
8. Hallatt & Lipa, p. 30
9. Hallatt & Lips, p. 35
10. Hallatt & Lipa, p. 29
11. Hallatt & Lipa, p. 26
12. Better Homes & Gardens, p. 32
13. Hallatt & Lipa, p. 25
14. Hallatt & Lipa, p. 8
15. Hallatt & Lipa, p. 27
16. Hallatt & Lipa, p. 32
17. Hallatt & Lipa p. 34
18. Farnham, Janice, personal communication
"(legacy)" Recipes: Based on entries from the private, transcribed, recipe collection of a former Fort Niagara cook who used the fireplaces and ovens of the French Castle and Bakehouse.

• Bibliography •

Armour, David A. and Widder Keith R. *At the Crossroads: Michilimackinac During the America Revolution.* Mackinac Island, MI: Mackinac Island State Park Commission, 19878.

Benson, Adolph B. (ed.). *Peter Kalm's Travels in North America: The English Version of 1770.* New York: Wilson-Erickson, Inc., 1937.

Bethune, Joanna. *The Unpublished Letters and Correspondence of Isabella Graham for the Years 1767 to 1814.* New York: John S. Taylor, 1838.

Better Homes and Gardens® Heritage Cookbook. United States of America: Meridith Corporation, 1975.

Billings, John D. *Hard Tack and Coffee: the Unwritten Story of Army Life,* Corner House Publishers, Williamstown, Massachusetts, 1973.

Bowler, R. Arthur. *Logistics and the Failure of the British Army in America, 1775-1783.* Princeton, NJ: Princeton University Press, 1975.

Bowler, R. Arthur (ed.). *A New System of Domestic Cookery by a Lady: Mrs. Maria Eliza Rundell's Original 1806 Classic.* Youngstown, NY: Old Fort Niagara Association, Inc. 1998.

Bowman, Georgianne, Editor. *1860's Foods; Union, Confederate & on the Frontier.* Online posting. 7 April 2001. <www.suite.101.com>.

Burgoyne, Bruce E. *A Hessian Diary of the American Revolution by Johann Conrad Döhla: From the 1913 Bayreuth Ed. by W. Baron Von Waldenfels.* Norman and London, University of Oklahoma Press, 1990.

Burgoyne, Bruce E. *Enemy Views: The American Revolutionary War as Recorded by the Hessian Participants.* Bowie, MD: Heritage Books, Inc., 1996.

Burgoyne, Bruce E. *Georg Pausch's Journal and Reports of the Campaign in America.* Bowie, MD: Heritage Books, Inc., 1996.

Carlo, Joyce W. *Trammels, Trenchers, & Tartlets: A Definitive Tour of the Colonial Kitchen.* Old Saybrook, CT: Peregrine Press, 1982.

Bibliography (continued)...

Chalmers, Margaret Taylor. *Colonial Fireplace Cooking & Early American Recipes.* East Lansing, MI: Shoestring Press, 1979.

Chartrand, René. *The French Soldier in Colonial America.* Bloomfield, Ontario: Museum Restoration Service, 1984.

Child, Mrs. *The American Frugal Housewife.* (1833) Cambridge, MA: Applewood Books, n.d.

Civil War Interactive. *The CWi Civil War Cookbook.* Online posting. 8 August 2002. <http://civilwarinteractive.com/cookbook.htm>.

Cometti, Elizabeth. (ed.). *The American Journals of Lt. John Enys.* Syracuse: Syracuse University Press. 1976.

Cormier-Boudreau, Marielle & Gallant, Melvin. *A Taste of Acadie.* Fredericton, New Brunswick: Goose Lane Editions, 1991.

Cruikshank, E.A. (ed.). *Records of Niagara: The First Settlement.* Niagara-on-the-Lake, Ontario: Niagara Historical Society, 1927.

Crump, Nancy Carter. *Hearthside Cooking.* McLean, VA: EPM Publications, Inc. 1986.

Cuthbertson, Bennett. *A System for the Complete Interior Management and Oeconomy of a Battalion of Infantry.* London: J. Millan, 1779.

David, Elizabeth. *English Bread and Yeast Cookery.* Harmondswark, England: Penguin Books, Ltd. 1977.

Drive, Christopher and Berriedale-Johnson, Michelle. *Pepys at Table: Seventeenth Century Recipes for the Modern Cook.* Berkeley, CA: University of California Press, 1984.

Duncan, Dorothy. *Serve it Forth!* Toronto: The Ontario Historical Society, Toronto, Ont. 1984.

Dunnigan, Brian Leigh. *A History and Guide to Old Fort Niagara.* Youngstown, NY: Old Fort Niagara Association, Inc. 1985

Dunnigan, Brian Leigh. *"The Necessity of Regularity in Quartering Soldiers" A Report to Mackinac State Historic Parks for the Exhibitions: Enemies to Allies, Cultural Accommodations in the Western Great Lakes, 1760-1783.* 1995.

Bibliography (continued)...

Dunnigan, Brian Leigh. *Memoirs on the Late War in North America Between France and England by Pierre Pouchot.* Youngstown, NY: Old Fort Niagara Association, Inc., 1994.

Encyclopediapopcornica. "RE: Popcorn." Online posting. 27 March 2001. <hww.popcorn.org/encyclopedia/eppophs.cfm>.

Eustice, Sally. *History from the Hearth.* Mackinac Island, MI: Mackinac State Historic Parks, 1997.

Farmer, Dennis & Farmer, Carol. *The King's Bread, 2nd Rising.* Youngstown, NY: Old Fort Niagara Association, Inc., 1989.

Frey, Sylvia R. *The British Soldier in America, A Social History of Military Life in the Revolutionary Period.* Austin, TX: University of Texas Press, 1981.

Fisher, Jabez M. Manuscript journal of Jabez M. Fisher, June, July 7 August 1773. Oneida historical Society, Utica, NY.

Fitch, Jabez Jr. *The Diary of Jabez Fitch Jr in the French and Indian War., 1757.* Glens Falls, NY: Rogers Island Historical Assoc., 1968.

Flick, Alexander, C. "New Sources on the Sullivan-Clinton Campaign in 1779." Reprinted from *Quarterly Journal of the New York State Historical Assoc.,* July & October, 1929.

Forsyth, George. Manuscript account book, 1780, RG10, Vol. 1838. National Archives of Canada, Ottawa, Ontario.

Gage, Thomas. Manuscript papers of General Thomas Gage, 1759-1775. William L. Clements Library, Ann Arbor, MI.

Glasse, Hannah. *The Art of Cookery, Made Plain and Easy.* Schenectady, NY: United States Historical Research Source, 1st edition 1745; Revised 1796; Reprinted 1994.

Gowan, Hugh & Gowan, Judy. *The Open Hearth.* Martinsburg, PA: Daisy Publications, 1987.

Gray, Paula. "Great Grains for Breakfast." Online posting. 14 March 01. <http://www. coopfoodstore.com /pages/topics/grains/html>

Bibliography (continued)...

Grose, Frances. *A Dictionary of Buckish Slang, University Wit, and Pickpocket Eloquence.* London: C. Chappel, 1811. Reprinted as *1811 Dictionary of the Vulgar Tongue.* Northfield, IL: Digest Books, 1971. The 1811 edition was taken almost entirely from Grose's *A Classical Dictionary of the Vulgar Tongue.* London, 1785.

Haldimand, Frederick. Manuscript papers of General Frederick Haldimand, Add. MSS 21661-21892. The British Library, London, England.

Hallatt, Mary Catherine & Lipa, Lynn M. The *King's Bread: Eighteenth Century Cooking at Niagara*. Youngstown, NY: Old Fort Niagara Association, Inc., 1986.

Huey, Paul R. "Animal Husbandry and Meat Consumption at Crown Point, New York in the Colonial Period and Revolutionary War." Unpublished Report, New York State Office of Parks, Recreation and Historic Preservation, Waterford, NY, 1979.

Innis, Mary Quayle (ed.). *Mrs. Simcoe's Diary.* Toronto: Macmillan of Canada Press, 1965.

Kahl, Bruce. "RE: Peas and Fat Chewing" Online posting. 16 May 01. <http://www.shu.ac/web-admin/phrases/bulletin_board/4/messages/1303.html>

Kent, Donald H. *The French Invasion of Western Pennsylvania, 1753.* Harrisburg, PA: Commonwealth of Pennsylvania History and Museum Commission, 1954.

Knox, John. *An Historical Journal of the Campaigns in North America for the Years 1757, 1758, 1759 and 1760.* Freeport, NY: Books for Libraries Press, 1970. Edited by Arthur G. Doughty.

Langton, H.H. (ed.). *Patrick Campbell: Travels in North America.* Toronto: Champlain Society, 1937.

Liebeman, Arthur. *Some Ecological Aspects of Northeastern American Indian Agroforestry Practices.* 1994 Annual reports of the Northern Nut Growers Association (vol.83) 3 July 01.<http://www.daviesand.corn/Papers/Tree_Crops/Indian_Agrforestry/>

Louisbourg Institute. *Behind the Scenes at the Fortress of Louisbourg.* 05/14/01. <http://w3.uccb.ns.ca/behind/broth.html>.

Lowell, Edward J. *The Hessian and the Other.* Williamstown, MA: Corner House Publishers, 1975.

Bibliography (continued)...

Luecke, Barbara K. *Feeding the Frontier Army, 1775-1865*. Eagan, MN: Grenadier Publications, 1990.

McFeely, George. Order book of Lt. Col. George McFeely, 1812-13. Archives of Ontario, Toronto, Ontario. Typed coped of the original.

McNair, James K. *All About Herbs*. San Ramon, CA: Ortho Books, 1973.

Mitchell, Patricia B. *French Cooking in Early America*. Chatham, VA, 1991.

Mitchell, Patricia B. *Revolutionary Recipes*. Chatham, VA, 2000.

Mitchell, Patricia B. *Union Army Camp Cooking*. Chatham, VA, 1994.

Parker, Arthur C. *"Iroquois Uses of Maize and other Food Plants."* New York State Museum Bulletin 144 No. 482. *Albany: New York State Museum. 1910.*

Rundell, Maria Eliza. See: Bowler, R. Arthur (ed.). *A New System of Domestic Cookery by a Lady.*

Sanderson, Capt. James M. *Camp Fires and Camp Cooking; or Culinary Hints for the soldier*. Washington Government Printing Office, 1862.

Sautai, Maurice. *Montcalm at the Battle of Carillon*. Ticonderoga, NY: Fort Ticonderoga Museum, 1914. Edited by John S. Watts.

Scott, Elizabeth M. *French Subsistence at Fort Michlimackinac, 1715-1781: The Clergy and the Traders*. Mackinac Island, MI: Mackinac Island State Park Commission, 1985.

Scott, Patricia and Scott, Stuart D. Unpublished preliminary listing of faunal remains recovered at Old Fort Niagara. copy in the Old Fort NIagara archeological project office.

Scott, Winfield. *General Regulations for the Army*. Philadelphia: M. Carey and Sons, 1821.

Simes, Thomas. *The Regulator or Instructions to Form the Officer and Complete the Soldier*. London, 1780.

Simmons, Amelia. *The First American Cookbook, A Facsimile of "American Cookery", 1796*. New York: Dover Publications, 1984.

Bibliography (continued)...

Simmons, Amelia. *American Cookery, 1796.* Green Farms, CT: The Silverleaf Press, 1984. Edited by Iris I. Frey.

Sloat, Caroline, *Old Sturbridge Village Cookbook.* Chester, CT: Globe Pequot Press, 1984.

Small, Harold A. ed., *The Road to Richmond: The Civil War Memoirs of Major Abner R. Small of the 16th Maine Volunteers,* Berkley, U. of California Press, 1939.

Stevens, Paul L. *A King's Colonel at Niagara, 1774-1776: Lt. Col. John Caldwell and the Beginnings of the American Revolution on the New York Frontier.* Youngstown, NY: Old Fort Niagara Association, Inc. 1987.

Stevens, S.K. et. al. (eds.). *The Papers of Henry Bouquet.* 5 vols.,; Harrisburg: The Pennsylvania Historical and Museum Commission, 1972-1984.

Sullivan, James and Hamilton, Miltn w. (eds.). *The Papers of Sir William Johnson,* 14 vols.; Albany: University of the State of New York, 1921-1965.

Syfert, Marguerite L. *From the Hearths at Fort Stanwix.* Rome, NY: Fort Stanwix, 1977.

Tonawanda Indian Baptist Church Cookbook. *'Heap Good Cookin' 125th Anniversary 1870-1995.* Basom, NY: Members and Friends of the Tonawanda Indian Baptist Church, 1995.

Weld, Isaac Jr. *Travels through the States of North America and the Provinces of Upper and Lower Canada during the years 1796, 1796, and 1797.* New York: Augustus M. Kelly Publisher, 1970.

Wheaton, Barbara Ketchum. *Savoring the Past: The French Kitchen and Table from 1200 to 1789.* Philadelphia: The University of Pennsylvania Press, 1983.

Wiley, Bell Irvin. *The Life of Billy Yank: The Common Soldier.* New York, Doubleday, 1952.

Wilson, Bruce G. *The Enterprise of Robert Hamilton.* Toronto: Carelton University Press, Inc., 1987.

Wood, Emma. *Antique Dinner Recipes for All Seasons.* Mount Vernon, NY: Constantia Books, 1987.

Wright, Louis B. and Tinling, Marlow (eds.). *Quebec to Carolina in 1785-1786, Being the Travel Diary and Observations of Robert Hunter, Jr. a Young Merchant of London.* San Marino, CA: The Huntington Library, 1943.

• Acknowledgements •

This cookbook would not have been possible without the expertise of so many people involved with Old Fort Niagara throughout the years.

Certainly the authors of the original book, *Mary Catherine Hallatt* and *Lynn M. Lipa* for their early work on *The King's Bread*. *Delores and Robert Pingitore* who, through their time and effort in developing the program and introducing the staff to eighteenth century cookery, guided Mary Catherine and Lynn. The authors of the second book, *The King's Bread, 2nd Rising* – Dennis and Carol Farmer – spent numerous hours providing a research base to the original recipes, as well as adding more recipes. Archeologists *Patricia and Stuart Scott* assisted in helping with which foods were eaten through their investigation of the faunal remains which were excavated during their years at Fort Niagara. The late *Marbud Prozeller* – a dedicated member of the archaeology staff – and *Joe Lee*, of Garden City, Michigan, created many of the illustrations used in all three books. Past Executive Director, *Brian Leigh Dunnigan* compiled much of the original primary source material that serves as the basis for programs at Old Fort Niagara.

Since the author has been at Old Fort Niagara, she has had assistance from various Old Fort Niagara persons-both volunteer and staff. *Jean Britten,* who served as the head of the distaff until the 2000 season, greatly influenced much of the cooking which was done by the author and other people in the bakehouse. Additional thanks go to *Yvonne Martin, Jan Czech* and *Judy Hannah*.

Lastly, thanks to *Harry M. DeBan*, Chairman of the Old Fort Niagara Publications Committee, who not only encouraged the author to attempt this endeavor, but brought about the production of *Pease Porridge,* through his expertise in layout and design.

• • • • • • • • • • • • • •

PRESERVING HISTORY AT
OLD FORT NIAGARA

Since 1927, the preservation and interpretation of Old Fort Niagara have been the goals of the Old Fort Niagara Association, Inc. The Association is a private, not-for-profit organization. Membership is open to anyone with an interest in the Fort and its long history. The Association operates Old Fort Niagara, a State Historic Site and National Historic Landmark, in cooperation with the New York State Office of Parks, Recreation and Historic Preservation.

Publications are an extension of the Association's educational purpose. The Publications Committee has been charged with establishing and maintaining an ongoing program of works relevant to the history of Old Fort Niagara. This includes new titles, as well as the republication of older works.

Additional information about the Fort's publications, exhibits, programs, or membership in the Old Fort Niagara Association may be obtained from:

Old Fort Niagara
Fort Niagara State Park
PO Box 169
Youngstown, New York 14174-0169

About the Author :

JoAnn Demler has enjoyed the role of interpreting the rich history of Old Fort Niagara since 1992. She is a member of the Old Fort Niagara Interpretive Volunteer Program and has enjoyed working out of the Bakehouse, as well as taking care of the garden. She has also worked as a seasonal distaff member.

JoAnn has been a teacher for more than 25 years, and holds a B.S. Degree in Education from the State University of New York College at Fredonia, an M.S. Degree in Special Education from the State University of New York College at Buffalo, and a New York State School District Administrator's Certificate. She currently teaches a study skills course for sixth grade students at Edward Town Middle School in the Niagara-Wheatfield Central School District, and also acts as the coordinator for the Academic Learning Center there. In the past, she taught special education students, and worked as the district's "gifted programming" specialist.

As living-history portrayers, JoAnn and her husband, Dale, have enjoyed reenactmenting the role of a 1779 family who had been "sent down from Montreal to live at the Fort during the Summer." Dale is the Fort's *Hesse-Hanau* artillerist, while JoAnn portrays his French-Canadian wife who came along as a laundress. Their son, Jonathan, played the role of French-Canadian youngster, until turning 16, at which time he assumed the role of musician and soldier for the *Eighth (King's) Regiment of Foot.* The family is also very involved during special events and other activities at the Fort.

JoAnn has become a *well seasoned* eighteenth-century cook under the direction and guidance of many Old Fort Niagara friends: Carol Farmer, Carole Bloomquist, Kate Jurus, and Jean Britten (just to mention a few). Her previous experiences as a camper, and wife of a Boy Scout leader, made open hearth cooking something easily pursued as a reenactor of early American life. Among her other interests are sewing, flower arranging and working on school musicals.

"Pease Porridge: Beyond the King's Bread..."
• **Production Notes** •

Project Coordinator, Design & Layout: Harry M. DeBan
Editing: Dean F. Ulrich, JoAnn Demler, Harry M. DeBan
Editing Assistance: Henri Michel duLac
Production Assistance: David J. Bertuca; Dean F. Ulrich; James Egloff; John Egloff; Dale Demler; Jonathan Demler; Cynthia Liddell; Sue Allen; Stuart and Patricia Scott
Production Support: Lt.Col. and Mrs. Harry G. DeBan, USAF(ret.); Marty Abramson; Keith G. Kozminski, Ph.D., University of Virginia (Charlottesville); Thomas M. O'Donnell; Michelle Sunderlin

- -

Memorare . . . **Dean Ford Ulrich and Delores Pingitore**

- -

• **Old Fort Niagara Publications** •
Harry M. DeBan, Publisher
Editorial Board: David J. Bertuca, R. Arthur Bowler, Ph.D., Craig O. Burt, III, John Burtniak, David Caldwell, Patricia Rice